Day Trading Signals

2022

*The Best Guide to Buying and Selling
Signals
for Day Trading and Scalping*

Table of Contents

Chapter 4: Trend Indicator and Moving Average Buy/Sell Signals

Getting Started

Trading can be a profitable endeavor, but only if you know when to buy and sell.

In this guide I will share with you my secret buy and sell signals for trading that have made me significant profits. These signals have been proven to be very profitable over time and you'll be able to make money no matter which way the market moves.

Once you know when to buy and sell, you can take advantage of market moves to make money. That's what day trading is all about – making money off of short-term market movements. First we need to cover the basics of how to use buy and sell signals in a trading strategy, and then we'll get into the actual signals themselves.

How To Use Buy And Sell Signals In Trading

As a trader, it is important to have a clear understanding of what constitutes a buy or sell signal. There are various technical indicators that can be used to generate buy and sell signals. Some common examples include moving averages, Bollinger Bands, and RSI (relative strength index).

When using indicators to generate signals, it is important to use multiple indicators to confirm each other. For example, if the moving average crossover indicates a buy signal, wait for the RSI to also indicate oversold conditions before making a trade. This will help ensure that the signal is more reliable.

When day trading, it is important to have a clear strategy. This means knowing what signals you will look for in order to make a trade. It is also important to have strict risk management rules in place. This will help you minimize losses and maximize profits.

Here are some examples of how you could use buy and sell signals in your day trading strategy:

-If the moving average crossover indicates a buy signal, wait for the RSI to confirm oversold conditions before making a trade.

-If the MACD histogram indicates a buy signal, wait for price to break above the resistance level before making a trade.

-If the stochastic oscillator indicates a sell signal, wait for price to break below the support level before making a trade.

By following these simple steps, you can develop a profitable day trading strategy using buy and sell signals.

Chapter 1: RSI Buy and Sell Signals

What Is The RSI?

The Relative Strength Index (RSI) is a momentum oscillator that measures the speed and change of price movements. The RSI can be used to identify general trends as well as predicting potential trend reversals. The indicator is calculated using the average prices of a security's gains and losses over a given period of time, and will range between 0-100.

There are a number of different ways that the RSI can be used to generate buy and sell signals, in this chapter we will look at some of the most accurate methods for finding buy/sell signals using the RSI.

Which method you use will largely depend on your personal trading style. Experiment and backtest with different techniques until you find one (or more) that works best for you and your trading strategy.

How it works:

The RSI indicator is combined with a moving average to create a trading signal. When the RSI crosses above the moving average, it generates a buy signal. When the RSI crosses below the moving average, it generates a sell signal.

The moving average helps to filter out noise and provides a smoother representation of price action. The RSI is used to identify momentum. When the two indicators are combined, they can provide accurate buy and sell signals in any market conditions.

Recommended Settings:

- 14-period RSI

- 21 EMA (exponential moving average) or 20 VWMA(volume weighted moving average)

Buy Signal:

- The buy signal is generated when the RSI crosses above the moving average. This indicates that momentum is shifting to the upside and prices are likely to continue higher.

Sell Signal:

- The sell signal is generated when the RSI crosses below the moving average. This indicates that momentum is shifting to the downside and prices are likely to continue lower.

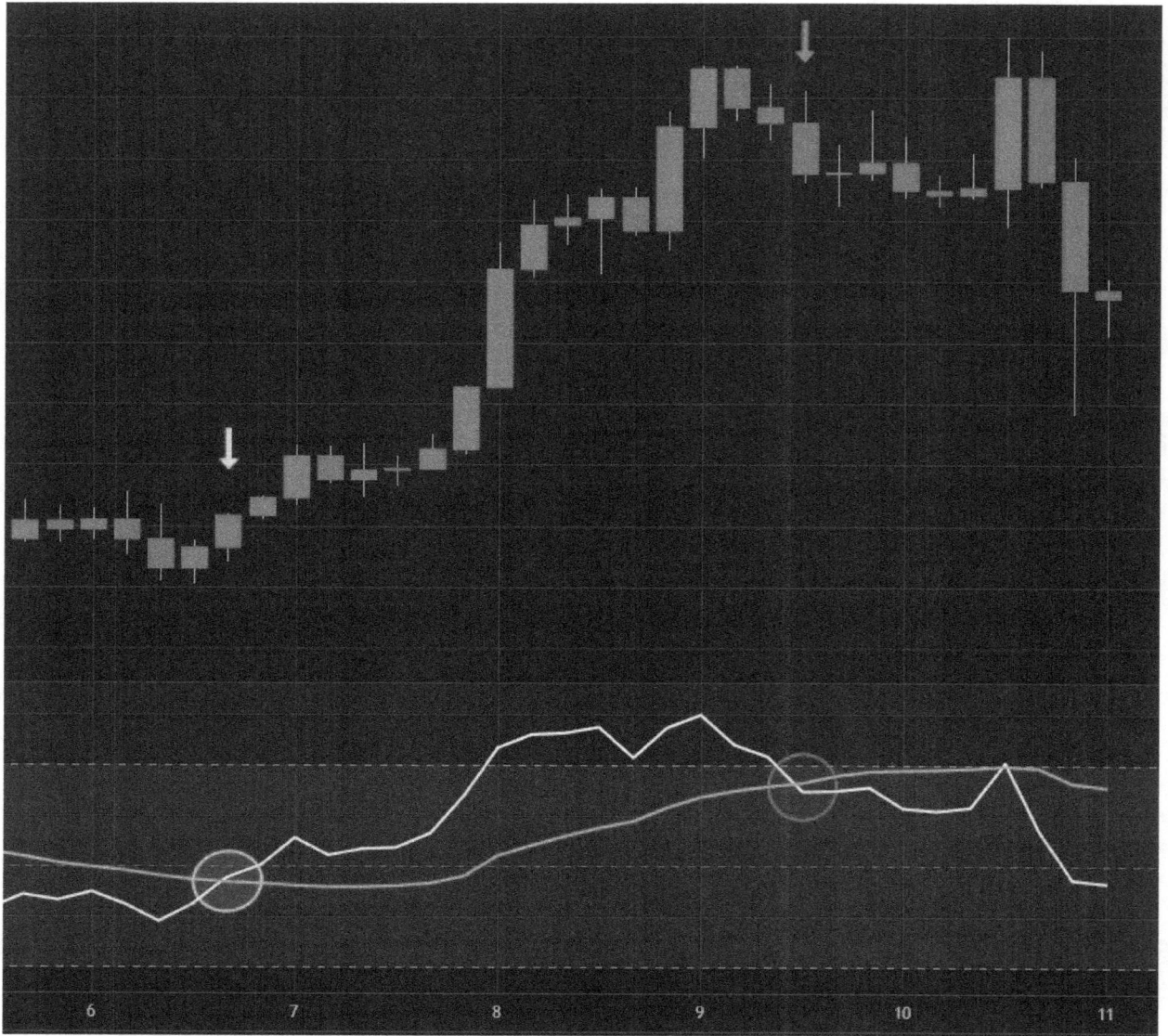

Example of buy (green circle) and sell (red circle) signals using this strategy

How it works:

Trend lines can be drawn on the RSI indicator to identify potential buy and sell signals. When the RSI crosses above a trend line, it generates a buy signal. When the RSI crosses below a trend line, it generates a sell signal.

Typically a trend line will break on the RSI before a trend reversal occurs in the market, this makes it a good leading indicator signal.

Recommended Settings:
- 21 period RSI

Buy Signal:
- The buy signal is generated when the RSI crosses above a downtrend line. This indicates that momentum is shifting to the upside and prices are likely to reverse higher.

Sell Signal:
- The sell signal is generated when the RSI crosses below an uptrend line. This indicates that momentum is shifting to the downside and prices are likely to reverse lower.

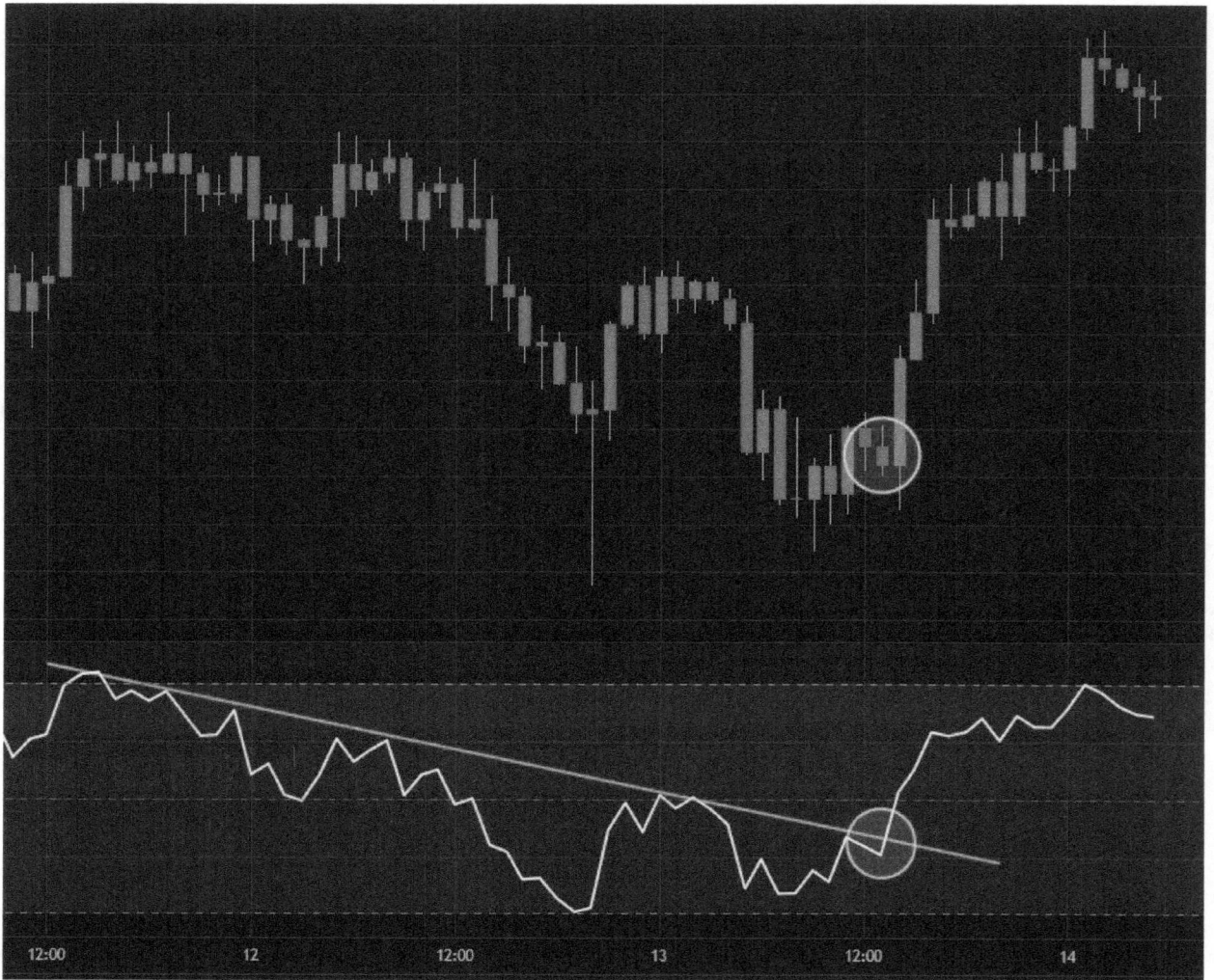

Example of a buy signal (green circle) using this method

RSI Buy/Sell Signal #3: RSI Oversold/ Overbought Signals

How it works:

This signal occurs when the market is overextended and is likely to have a pullback. If the RSI is oversold this indicates the market is overextended to the downside and is likely to bounce. Conversely if the RSI is overbought this signals that the market has risen too quickly and a pullback is likely.

Overbought/oversold signals work the best in rangebound, sideways moving markets. When the market is in a strong trend, overbought/oversold signals will be less reliable.

Recommended Settings:

- Change length to 5 or 7 for day trading and scalping
- A length of 14 is good for longer term swing trading strategies

Buy Signal:

- The RSI falls below 30
- Wait for the RSI to cross back above the oversold zone before using it for entries

Sell Signal:

- The RSI rises above 70
- Wait for the RSI to cross back below the overbought zone before using it as an exit signal.

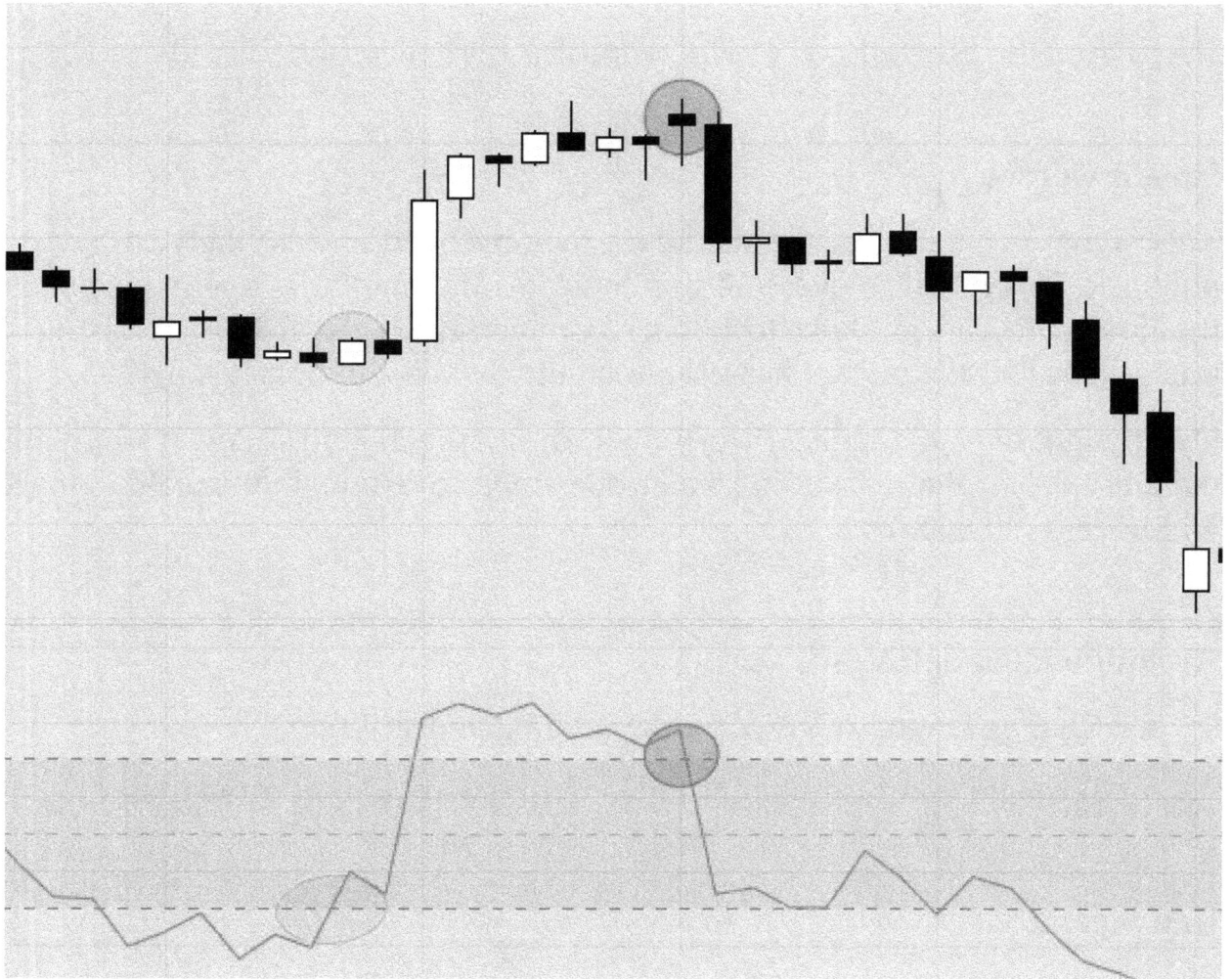

An example of overbought/oversold signals using a 5 period RSI

RSI Buy/Sell Signal #4: RSI Center Line Cross

How it works:

This signal occurs when the RSI crosses above or below the 50 level, this is sometime refered to as a "center line cross" signal. When the RSI crosses 50, this indicates a trend change is occurring.

If the RSI crosses above 50 this is a bullish signal and suggests prices are likely to continue to move higher.

Conversely, if the RSI crosses below 50 this is a bearish signal and indicates prices are likely to move lower.

50 level cross signals work best in trending markets but can also be used in rangebound or sideways moving markets.

Recommended Settings:

- 30 period RSI

Buy Signal:

- When the RSI crosses above 50

Sell Signal:

- When the RSI crosses below 50

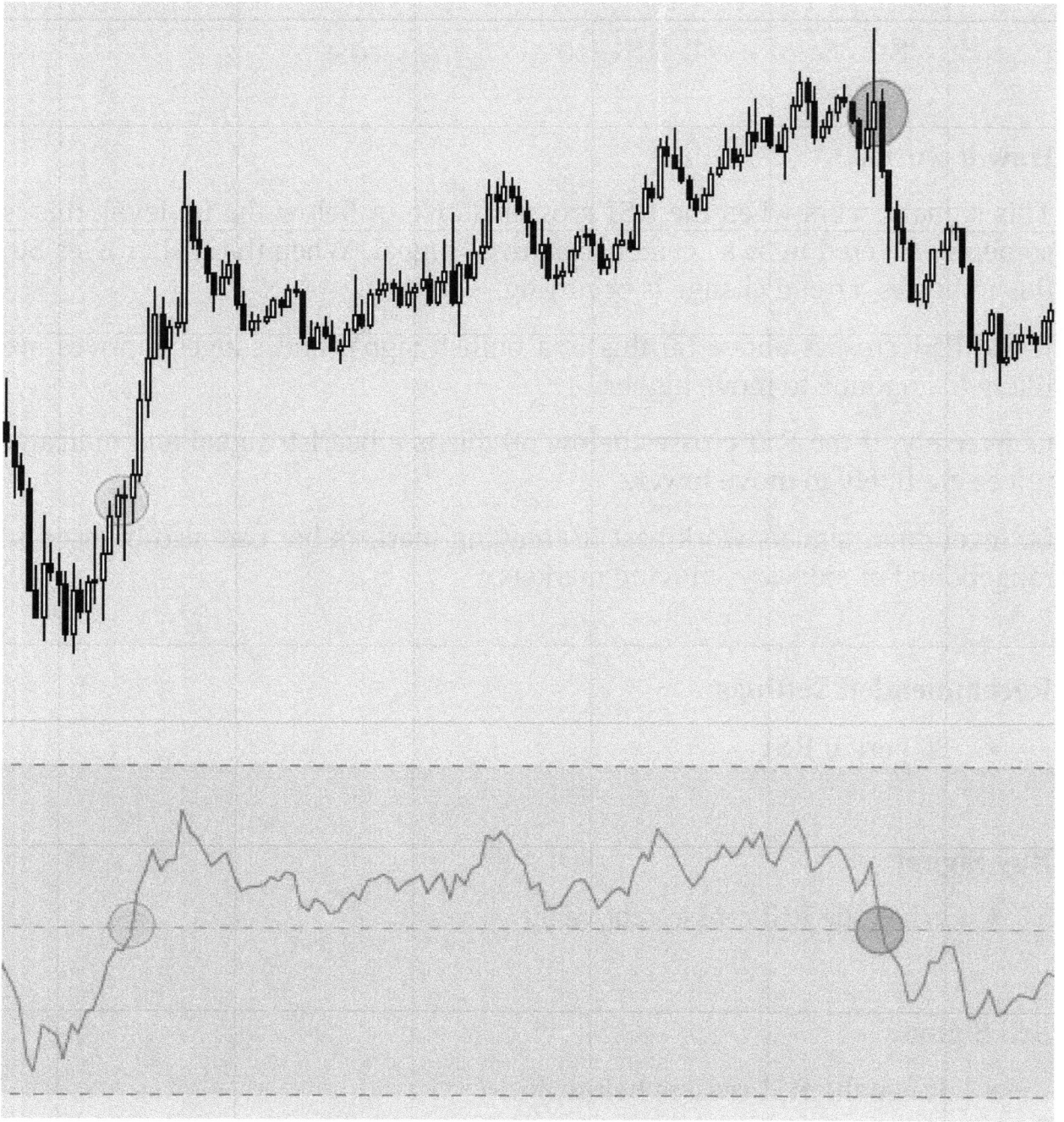

An example of a buy and sell signal

RSI Buy/Sell Signal #5: 2 Period RSI

How it Works:

This method uses a 2 period RSI to generate buy/sell signals. It is a very popular method among day traders. This strategy can be used to accurately identify short term momentum shifts in the market. Buy and sell signals will occur when the RSI moves above 70 or below 30.

This method is good for scalping due to the frequent signals.

Recommended Setting:
- 2 period RSI

Buy Signal:
- The buy signal is generated when the 2 period RSI crosses above 70

Sell Signal:
- The sell signal is generated when the 2 period RSI crosses below 30

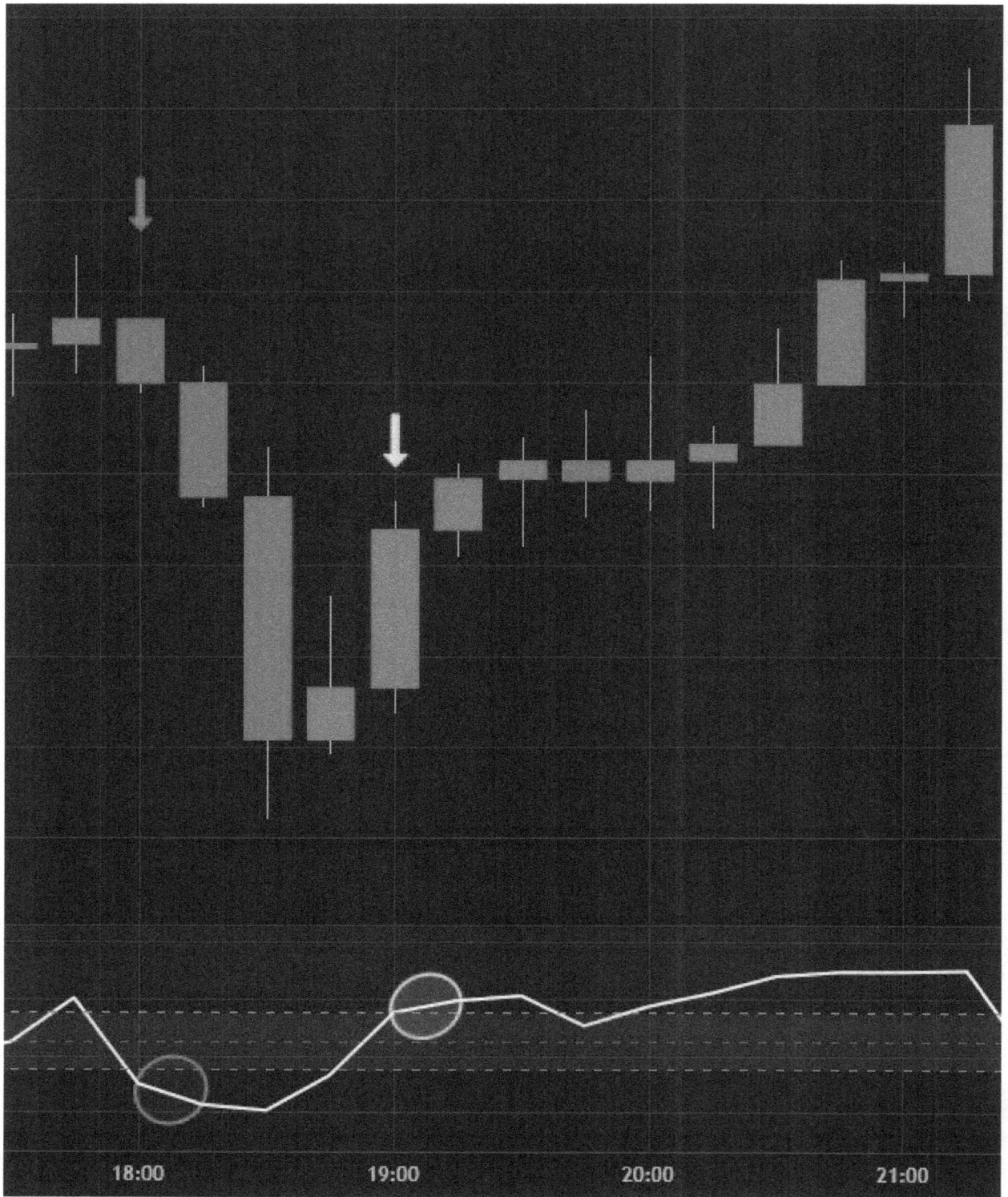

Example of a buy (green circle) and sell (red circle) signal using this method

Chapter 2: Bollinger Bands Buy/Sell Signals

What Are The Bollinger Bands and How Does It Work?

The purpose of the Bollinger Bands is to help traders identify when a security is over- or undervalued. In other words, it gives traders an idea of what is considered expensive or cheap in the market.

The Bollinger Bands can also be used as a volatility indicator and allow you to identify when the market is trading in a tight range, or when it is starting to trend.

Components of the Bollinger Band

The Bollinger Bands consists of upper and lower bands that are placed two standard deviations away from a simple moving average (known as basis line).

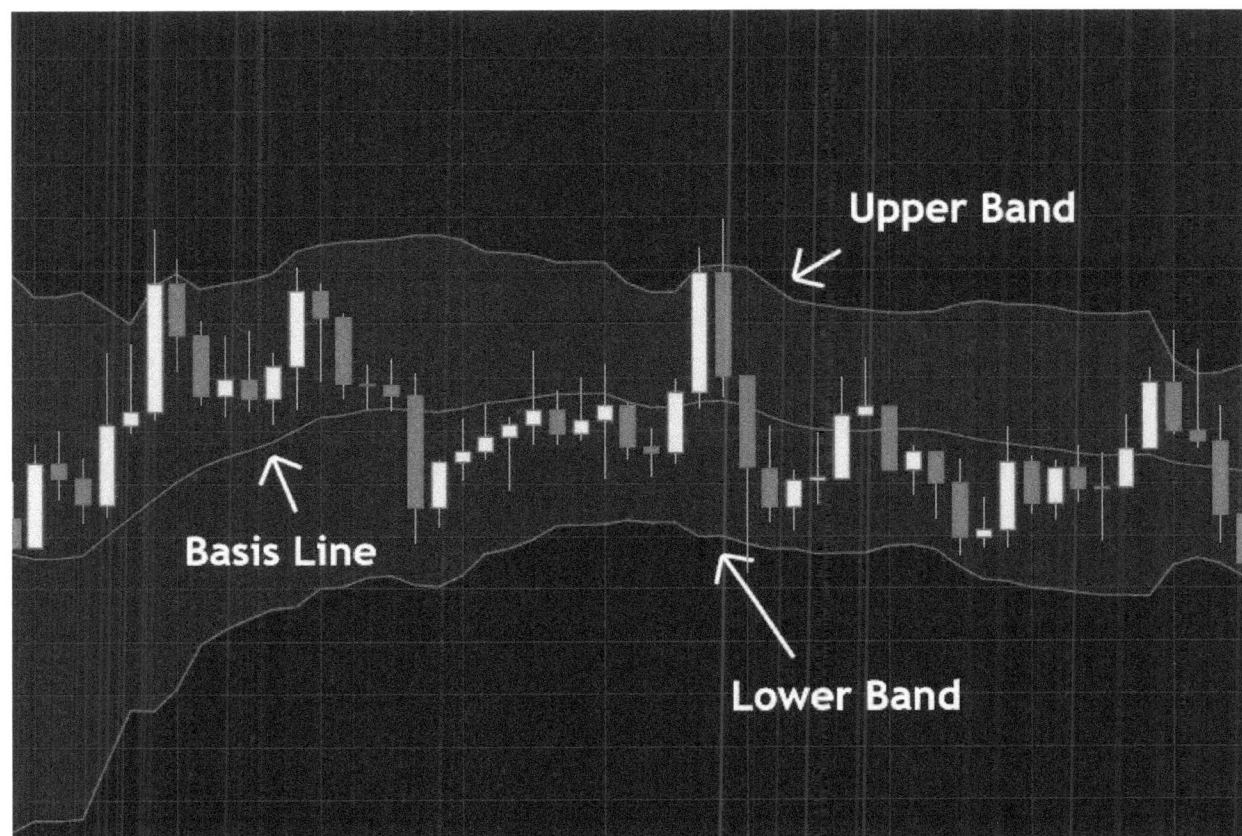

When prices are relatively high in relation to the upper Bollinger Band, it is considered overbought. This means that prices may be due for a correction or pullback. On the other hand, when prices are relatively low in relation to the lower Bollinger Band, it is considered oversold. This means that prices may be due for a rally.

The best time to trade Bollinger band crosses is when the market is relatively stable and there is no clear trend. This usually happens after a period of consolidation or range-bound trading.

The Bollinger Bands can also be used to confirm other signals. For example, if you see a bullish candlestick pattern forming at the same time that prices are moving below the lower Bollinger Band, this could be an indication that prices are about to start moving higher.

The Bollinger Band Squeeze

The space between the two lines is called the trading range. The width of the trading range can be used to show how volatile prices are. When volatility is high, the Bollinger Bands will be far apart, and when volatility is low, the Bollinger Bands will be close together.

When the Bollinger Bands are close together this is called a squeeze. The Bollinger Band squeeze is a good way to find trading opportunities as prices will break out of the squeeze, and begin trending. When this happens, it is usually best to wait until price breaks out - up or down before taking a trade.

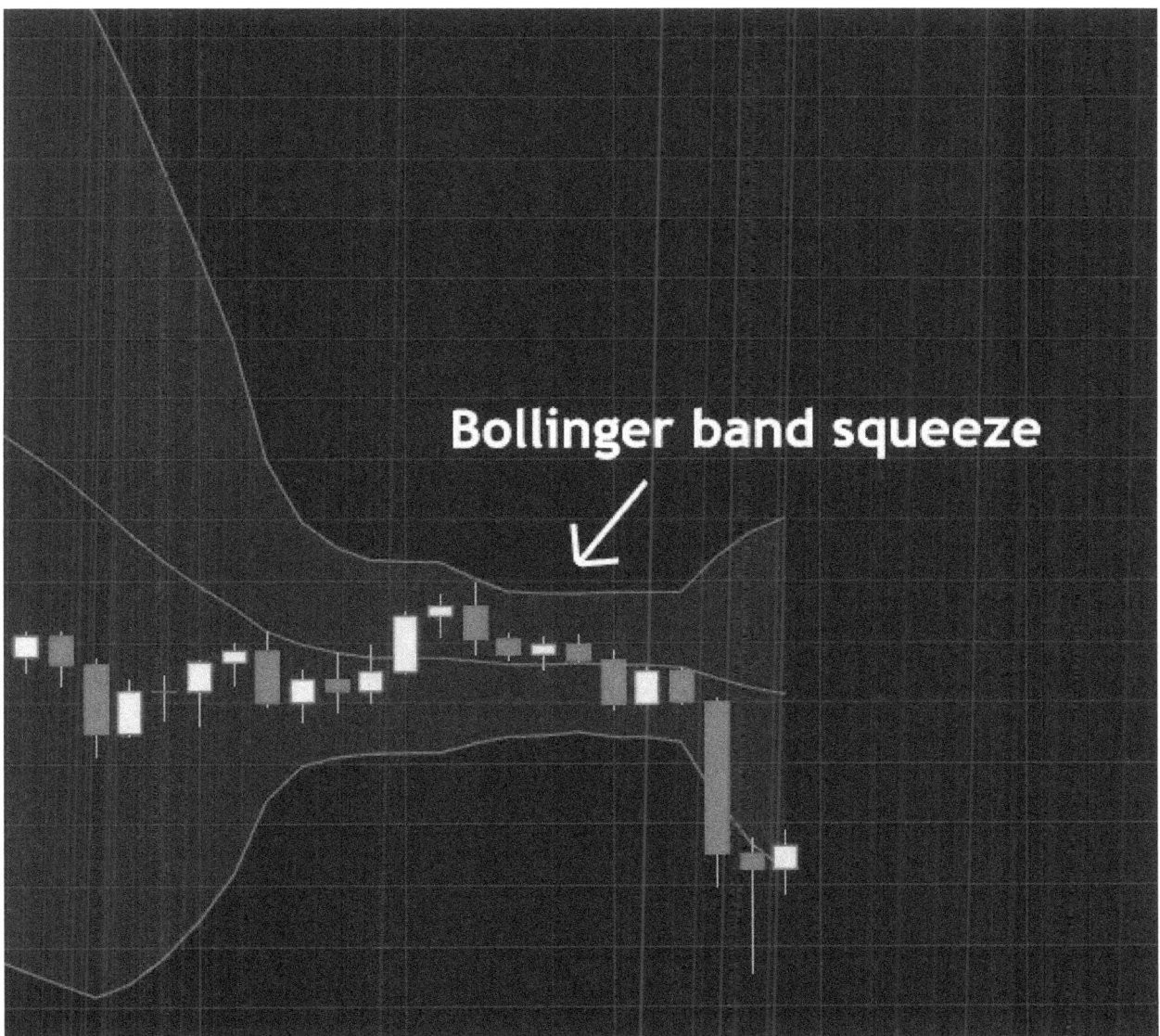

Bollinger band squeeze

Bollinger Bands Buy/Sell Signal #1: Price Crosses Upper/Lower Bands

How It Works:

When the price crosses above or below the upper or lower Bollinger Bands, it creates a buy/sell signal. When price crosses above the top or bottom band, this indicates price is overextended in a certain direction and it is likely to revert back to its mean (middle line).

Recommended Settings:

- Length = 20, Std dev = 2.2

- Length 25, Std dev = 2

- The default settings (Length = 20, Std dev = 2) also produce accurate signals

Buy Signal:

- Price crosses below the bottom Bollinger Band. This indicates that the price overextended to the downside and a bounce is likely.

Sell Signal:

- Price crosses above the upper Bollinger Band. This indicates that the price overextended to the upside and a pullback is likely.

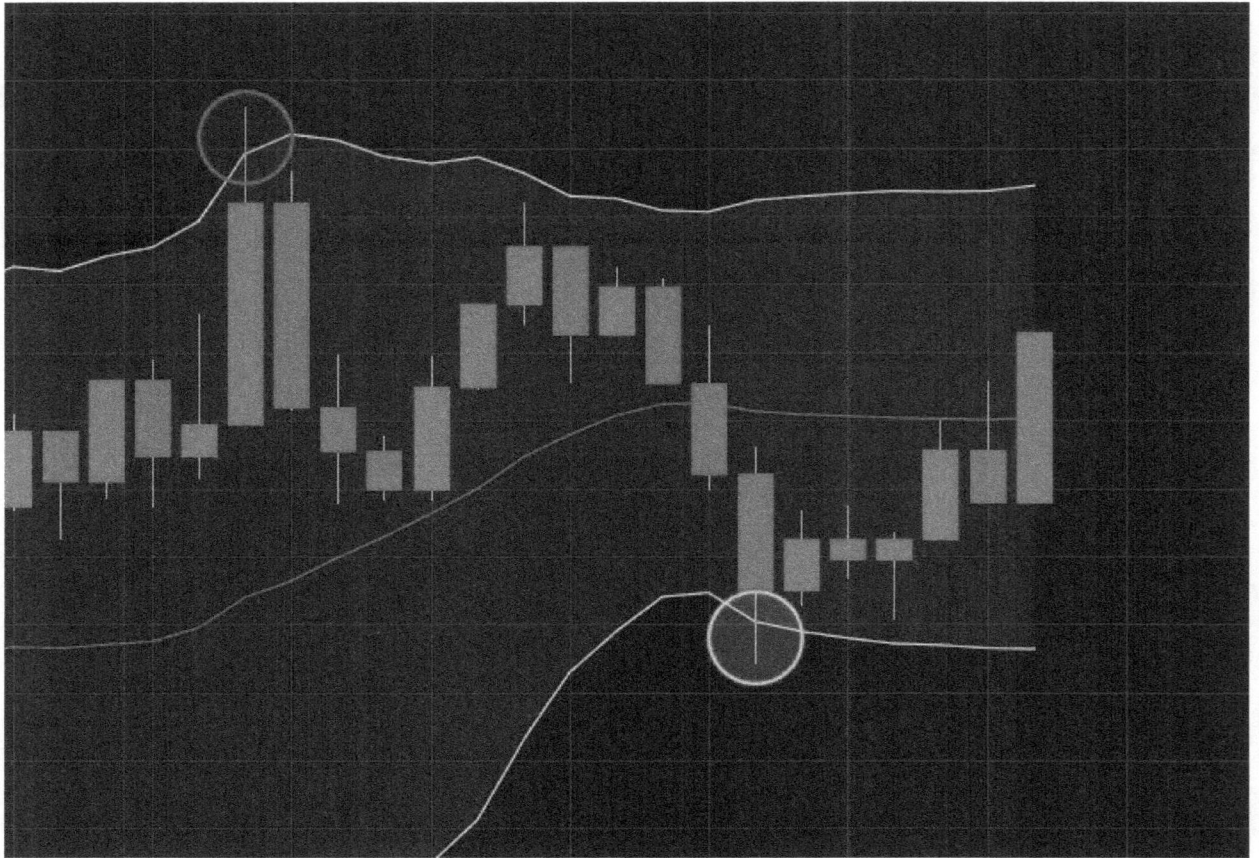

Example of a buy (green circle) and sell (red circle) using this method

How It Works:

A Bollinger Band Squeeze happens when the Bollinger Bands (upper and lower bands) narrow or "squeeze" together.

This indicates low volatility in the market and a potential breakout is about to occur. When the squeeze happens, the market is "coiling" for a move.

Recommended Settings:

- Length = 20, Std dev = 2.5

Buy Signal:

- A candle closes above the upper Bollinger Band while it is being squeezed. This indicates that a period of low volatility has ended and price is ready to start moving higher.

Sell Signal:

- A candle closes below the lower Bollinger Band whole it is being squeezed. This indicates that a period of low volatility has ended and price is ready to start moving lower.

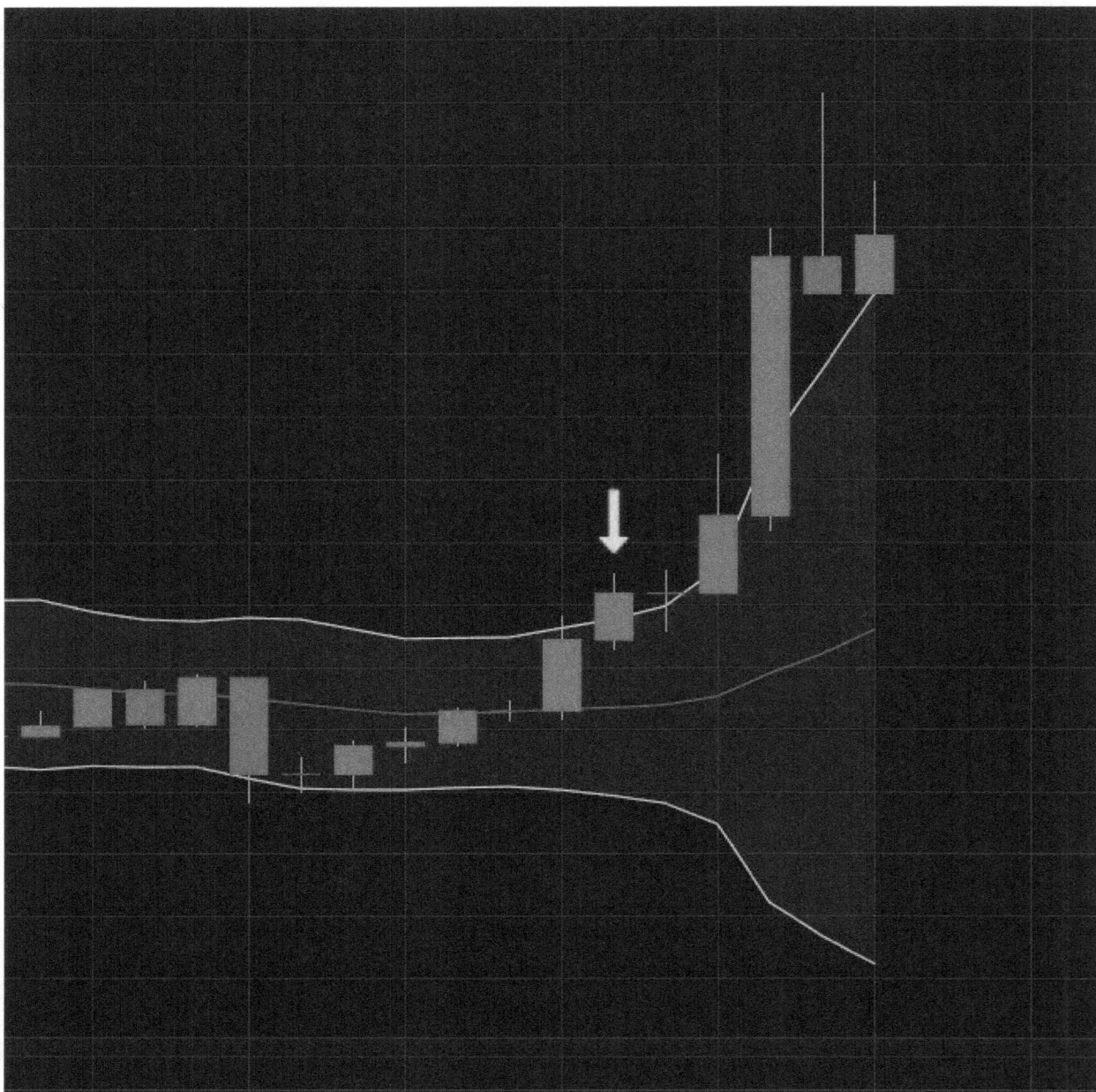

Example of a buy signal using this method

Bollinger Bands Buy/Sell Signal #3: Bollinger Band Trend Following System

How It Works:

This method changes the standard deviation of the Bollinger bands to 1, and uses price crossing above or below the bands to catch trending moves. Price will remain above/below the bands while a strong trending move is occurring.

Recommended Settings:

- Length = 50, Std dev = 1

Buy Signal:

- Price crosses above the upper Bollinger Band. This indicates that a strong uptrend is in place and price is likely to continue moving higher.

Sell Signal:

- Price crosses below the lower Bollinger Band. This indicates that a strong downtrend is in place and price is likely to continue moving lower.

Example of a buy signal (green circle) using this method

Bollinger Bands Buy/Sell Signal #4: Bollinger Bands + RSI

How It Works:

To use this signal you will need to add Bollinger bands onto the RSI. Signals will occur when the RSI moves above or below the Bollinger band. This method works well for scalping, day trading and swing trading.

Recommended Settings:

- 20-period Bollinger bands with 1 standard deviations

- 14-period RSI

Buy Signal:

- A buy signal is generated when the RSI crosses above the top Bollinger band. Exit long trade when it crosses back below the top Bollinger band

Sell Signal:

- A sell signal is generated when the RSI crosses below the bottom Bollinger band. Close short trade when it crosses back above it.

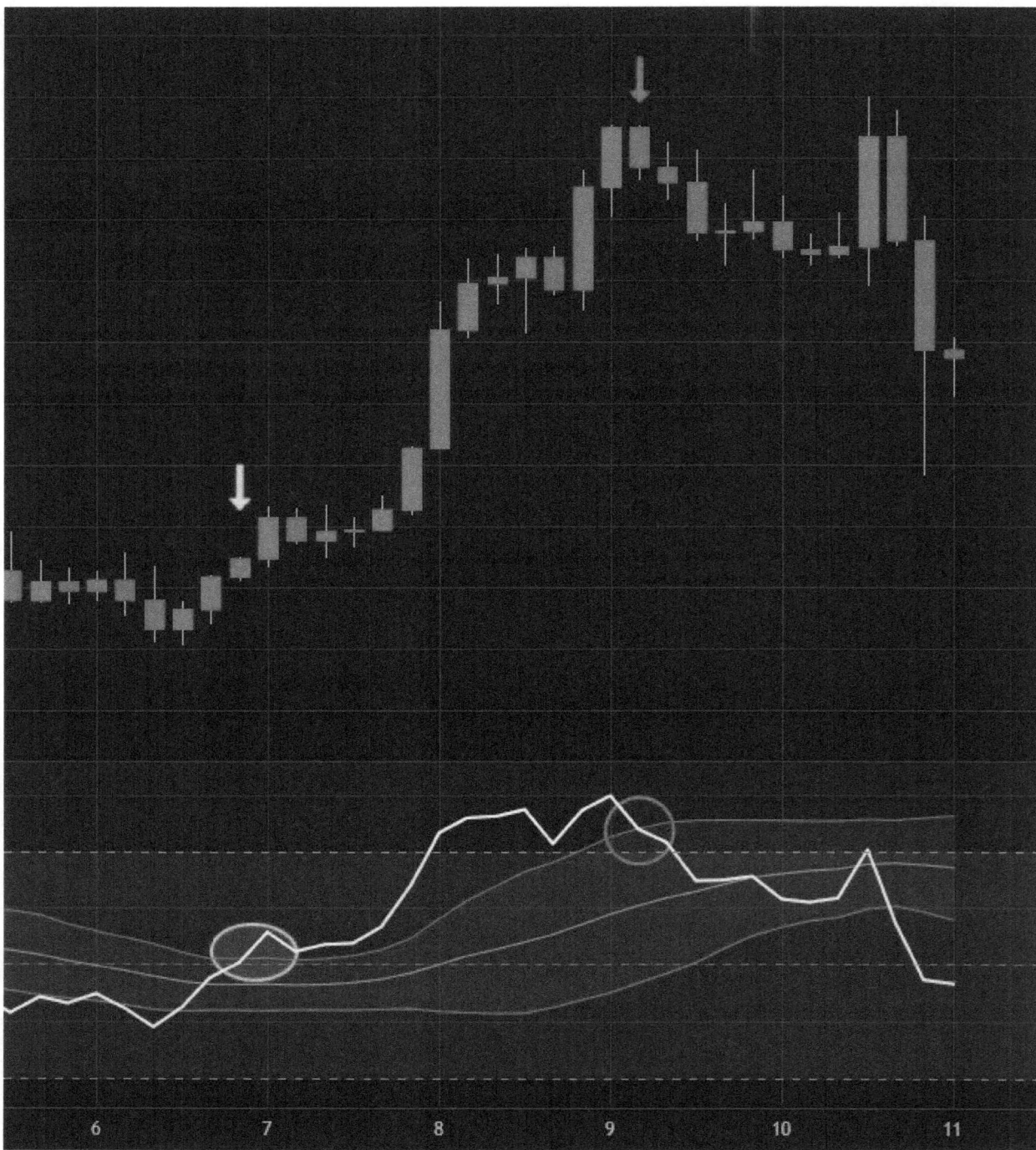

Example of a buy signal (green circle) using this method

Bollinger Bands Buy/Sell Signal #5: Bollinger Bands Slope + Middle Band

How It Works:

For this method the Bollinger bands must be sloped in one direction – either up or down. A signal occurs when price touches the middle band. The buy/sell signal will depend on the slope of the bands.

Recommended Settings:

Length = 20, Stdev = 2

Buy Signal:

- The Bollinger bands are slopped up, buy when price touches the middle band

Sell Signal:

- The Bollinger bands are slopped down, sell when price touches the middle band

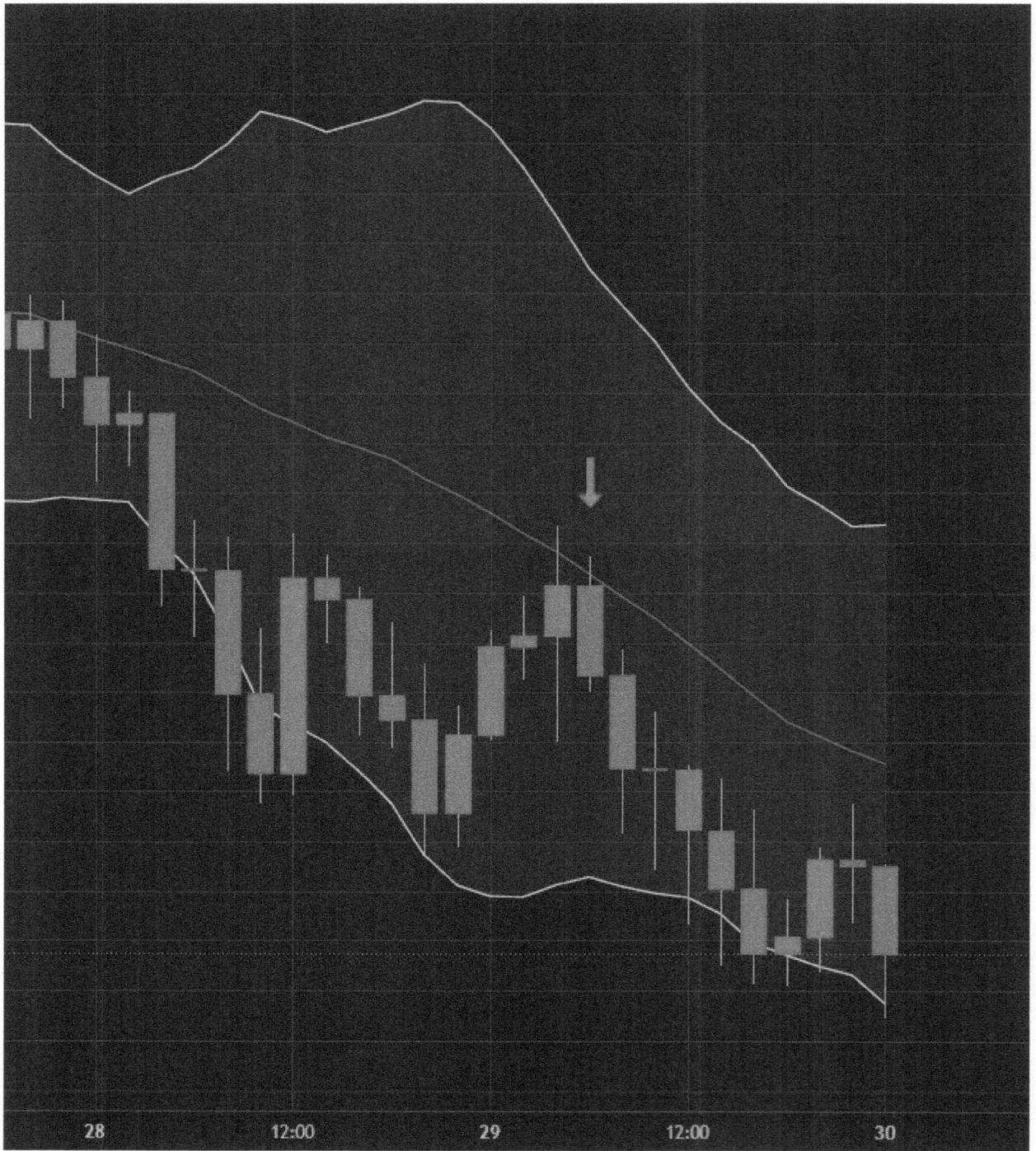

Example of a sell signal using this method

Chapter 3: Indicator Crossover Buy/Sell Signals

In this chapter, we'll take a look at some of the most profitable technical indicators and explore how you can use them to generate trading signals.

To find these indicators on TradingView:

- Go into the "Indicators & Strategies" window on

- Click on the "Community Scripts" tab.

- Type the name of the indicator in the search box

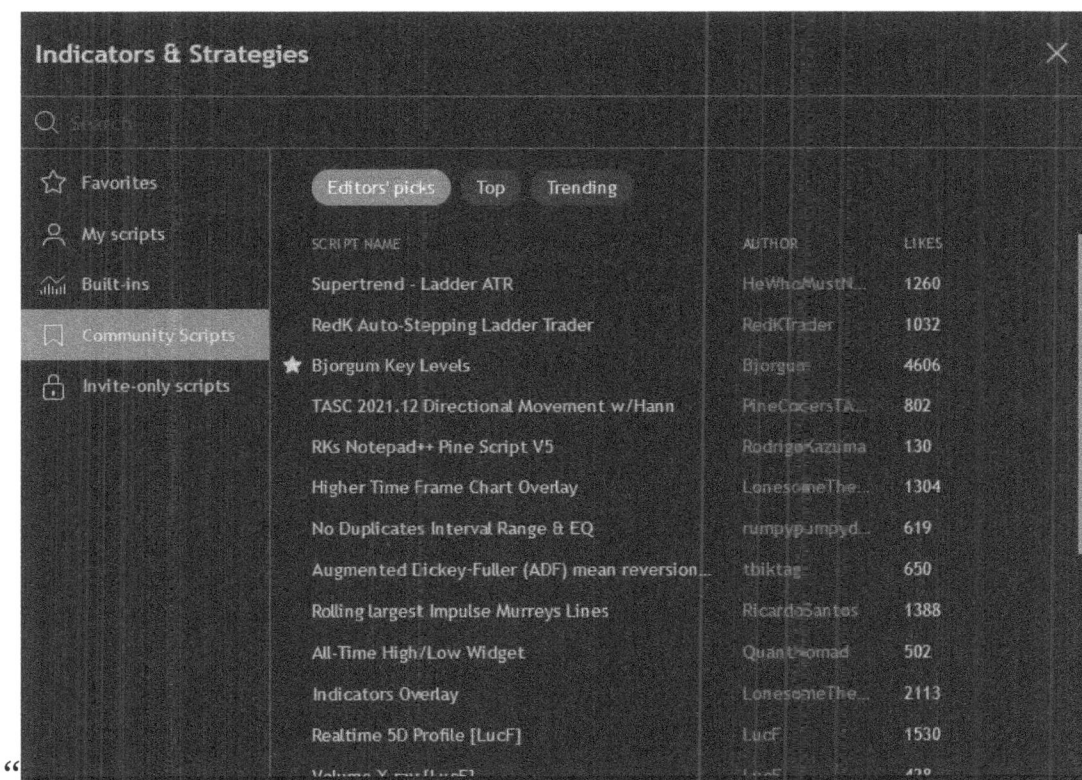

These indicators provide very accurate buy and sell signals, and are great for combining into a trading strategy.

Many of these signals are from indicators that the TradingView community has created.

Buy/Sell Signal #1: Scalp Pro

Author: ovelix

Search "Scalp Pro" in the indicator search box on TradingView to find this indicator (author – ovelix)

How it Works:

This indicator is based on modified MACD calculations and is displayed as a crossover oscillator with two lines, one fast and one slow (similar to a stochastic). Signals are generated when the fast line crosses above or below the slow line.

This indicator is great for scalping, it produces frequent signals most of which are accurate. The buy and sell signals will appear as labels on this indicator making it easy to use. This indicator works well in volatile market conditions.

Recommended Settings:

- Change the smooth length to 10 to reduce the amount of false signals

Buy Signal:

- The fast line crosses above the slow line and a green buy label appears

Sell Signal:

- The fast line crosses below the slow line and a red sell label appears

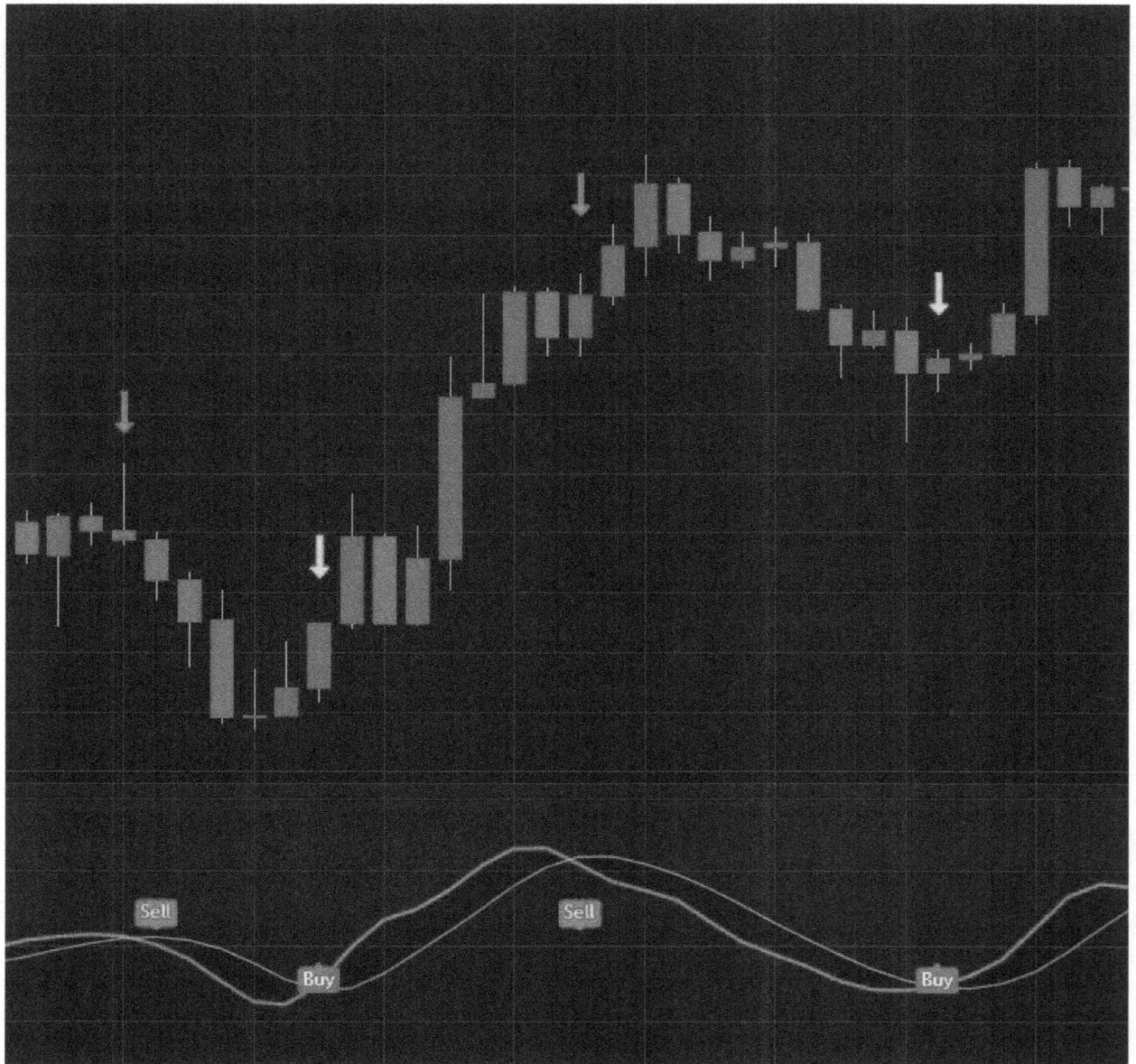

Example of buy (green arrow) and sell (red arrow) signals using this indicator

Buy/Sell Signal #2: MACD (improved settings)

What Is It?

This method uses the MACD indicator crossovers as buy/sell signals. The MACD is a momentum indicator that is based on two exponential moving averages.

This strategy changes the default settings of the MACD to produce more accurate buy/sell signals and filter out the bad signals that frequently occur with the default MACD settings.

Recommended Settings:

- Fast Length = 20, Slow Length = 50, Signal Smoothing = 21

Buy Signal:

- The fast MACD line crosses above the slow line

Sell Signal:

- The fast MACD line crosses below the slow line

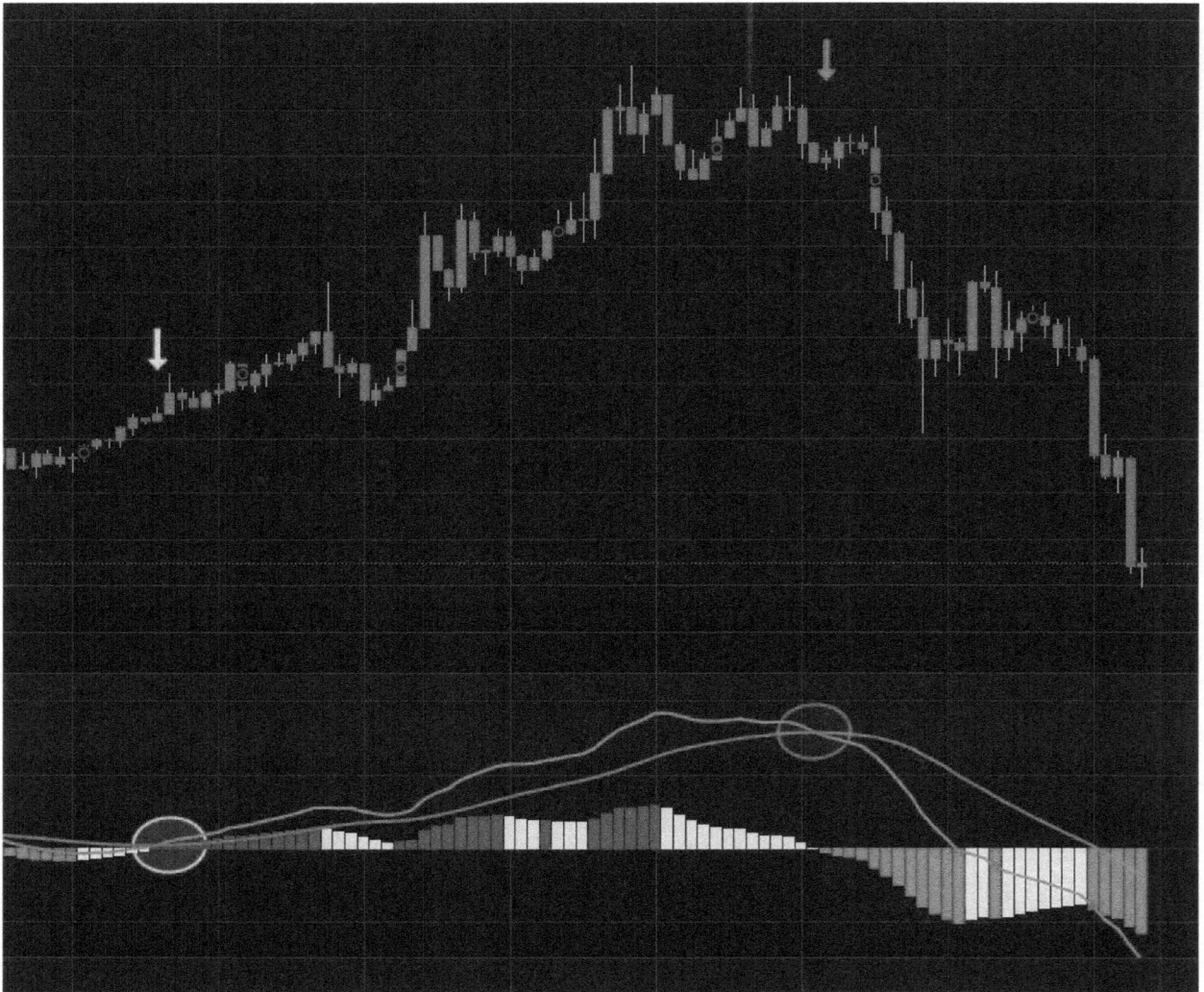

Example of buy (green circle) and sell (red circle) signals using this method

Buy/Sell Signal #3: Stochastic OTT

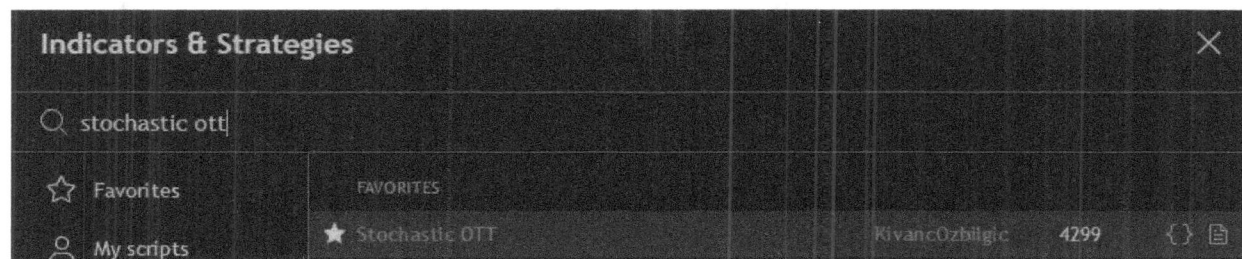

Search "Stochastic OTT" in the indicator search box on TradingView to find this indicator (author – KivancOzbilgic)

What is it?

This indicator is similar to the stochastic oscillator, but it combines the stochastic oscillator with the optimized trend tracker indicator. This reduces the false signals given by the stochastic oscillator that can be caused by volatile moves.

Recommended Settings

%K Length = 100, %K Smoothing = 10, OTT period = 2, OTT percent = 0.5

Buy Signal:

- When the fast line crosses above the slow line

Sell Signal

- When the fast line crosses below the slow line

Buy/Sell Signal #4: Normalized Smoothed MACD

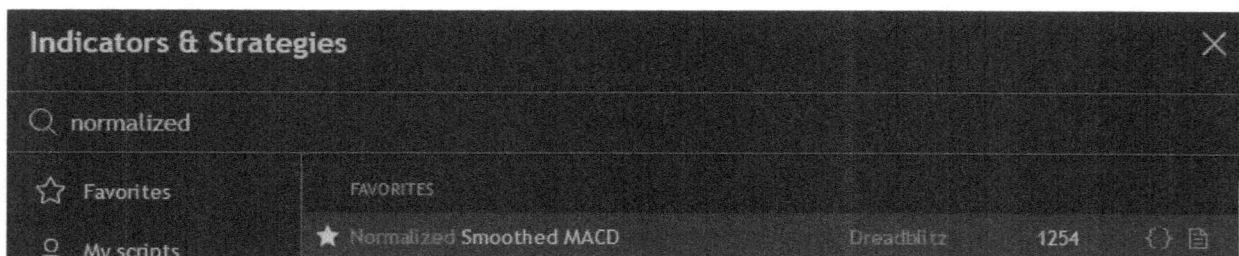

Search "Normalized Smoothed MACD" in the indicator search box on TradingView to find this indicator (author – Dreadblitz)

What is it?

This indicator is an improved version of the MACD indicator, and provides more reliable entry and exit signals then a regular MACD. Two lines are displayed on this indicator, the signal line and MACD line

Buy/Long Signal:

- The MACD line is below the zero line

- The MACD crosses above the signal line and the MACD line turns green

Sell/Short Signal:

- The MACD line is above the zero line and turns red

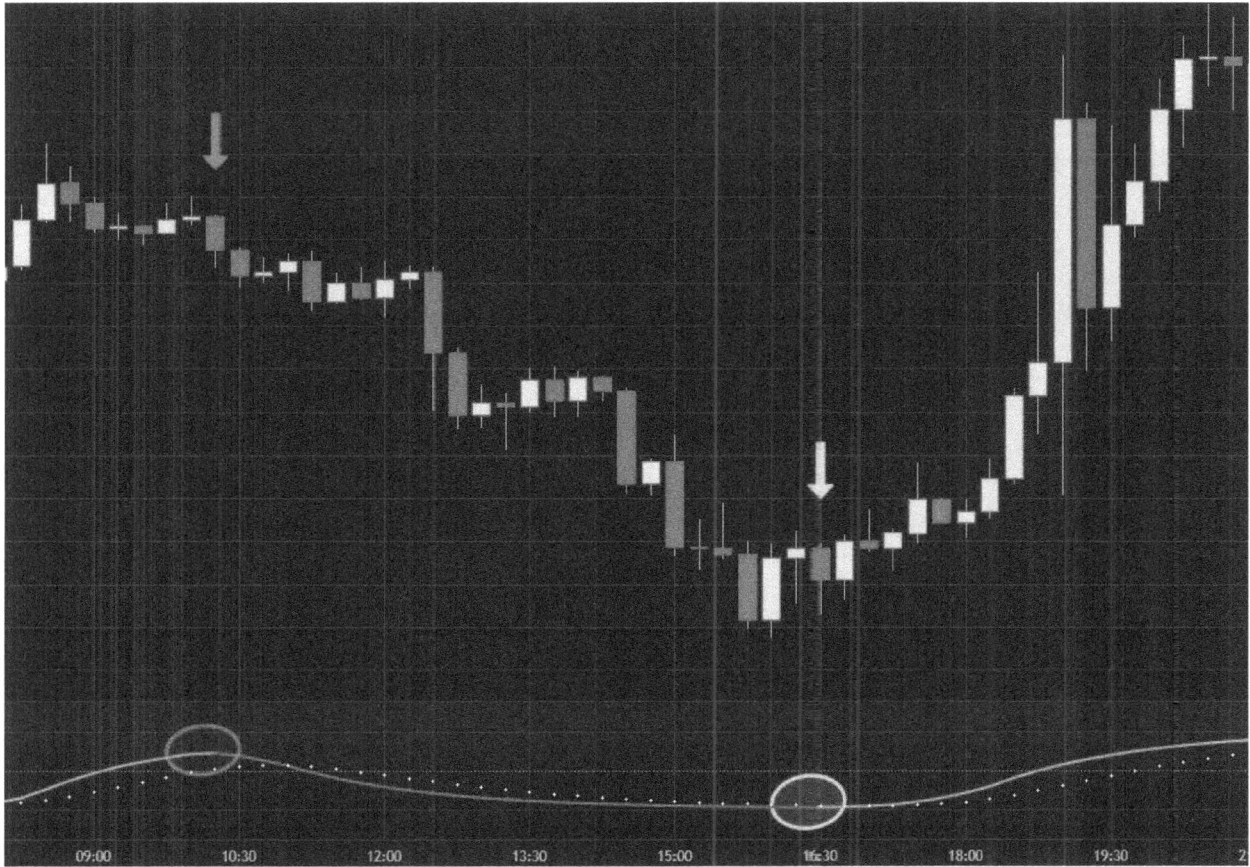

Example of entry and exit signals using this indicator

Buy/Sell Signal #5: Stochastic Weights - Basic

To find this indicator type in "Stochastic Weights - Basic", in the indicator search box on TradingView (author - BigBitsIO)

How it works:

This indicator is similar to a normal stochastics with a %K and %D line. When the stochastic moves above 80 it is considered overbought and below 20 is oversold. This indicator can give more accurate signals then a regular stochastic since it includes other values in its calculations.

Tip: I recommend enabling all of the stochastics in the indicator settings

Buy Signal:
- The %K line crosses above the %D line while under 50

Or

- The stochastic above 20 after being oversold

Sell Signal:

- The %K line crosses below the %D line while above 50

Or

- The stochastic crosses below 80 after being oversold

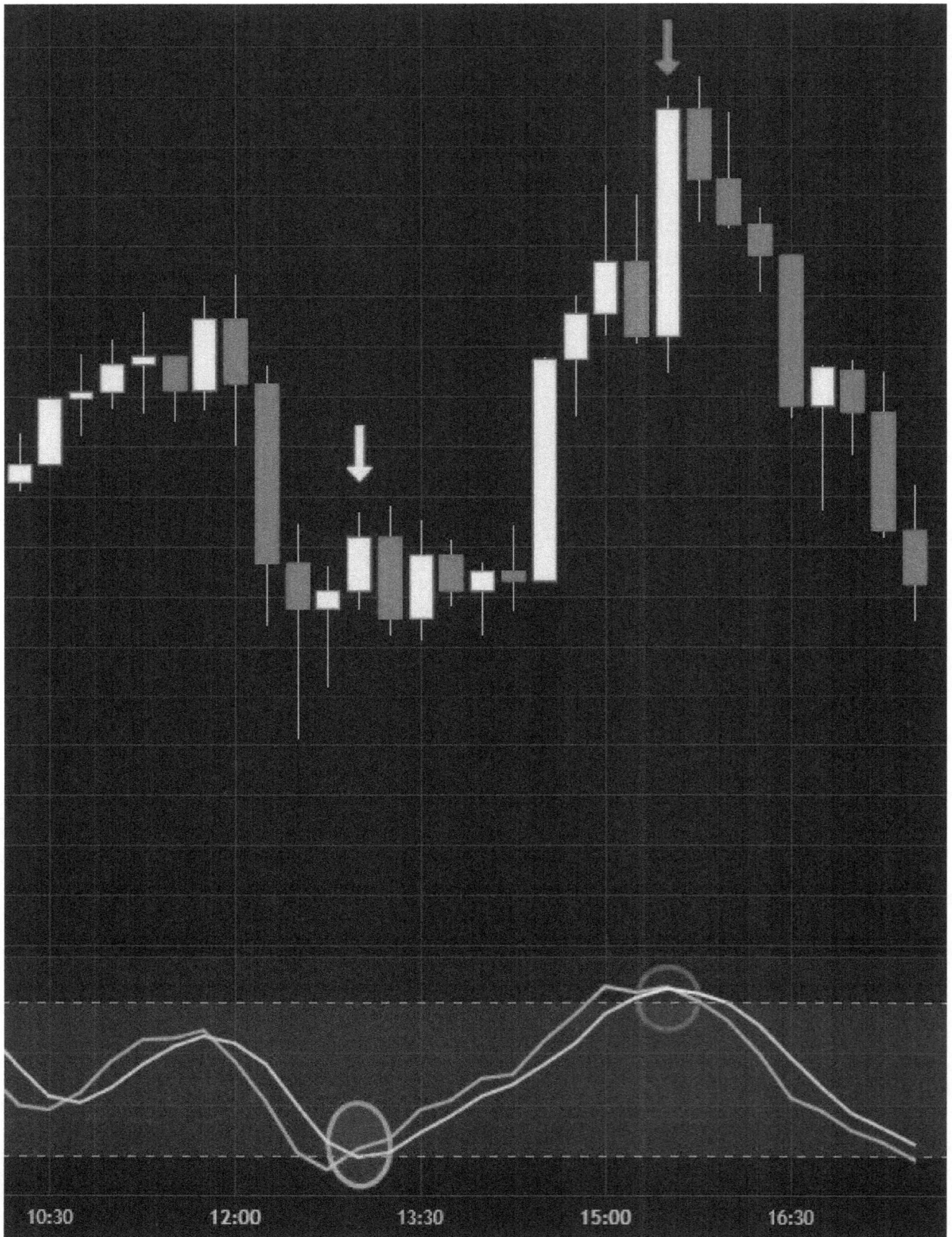

An example of buy (green arrow) and sell (red arrow) signals using this indicator

Buy/Sell Signal #6: RMI by Cobra

Search "RMI by Cobra" in the indicator search box on TradingView to find this indicator (author – binary_trader66)

What is it?

RMI (relative momentum index) is similar to the RSI and measures the momentum of a trend. This indicator has 2 lines, the RMI line and a slower moving average.

Buy/Long Entry Signal:

- When the fast line (RMI) crosses above the slower moving average

Or

- The RMI changes to blue color

Exit Long Signal

- When the fast line (RMI) crosses below the moving average

Or

- The RMI turns red

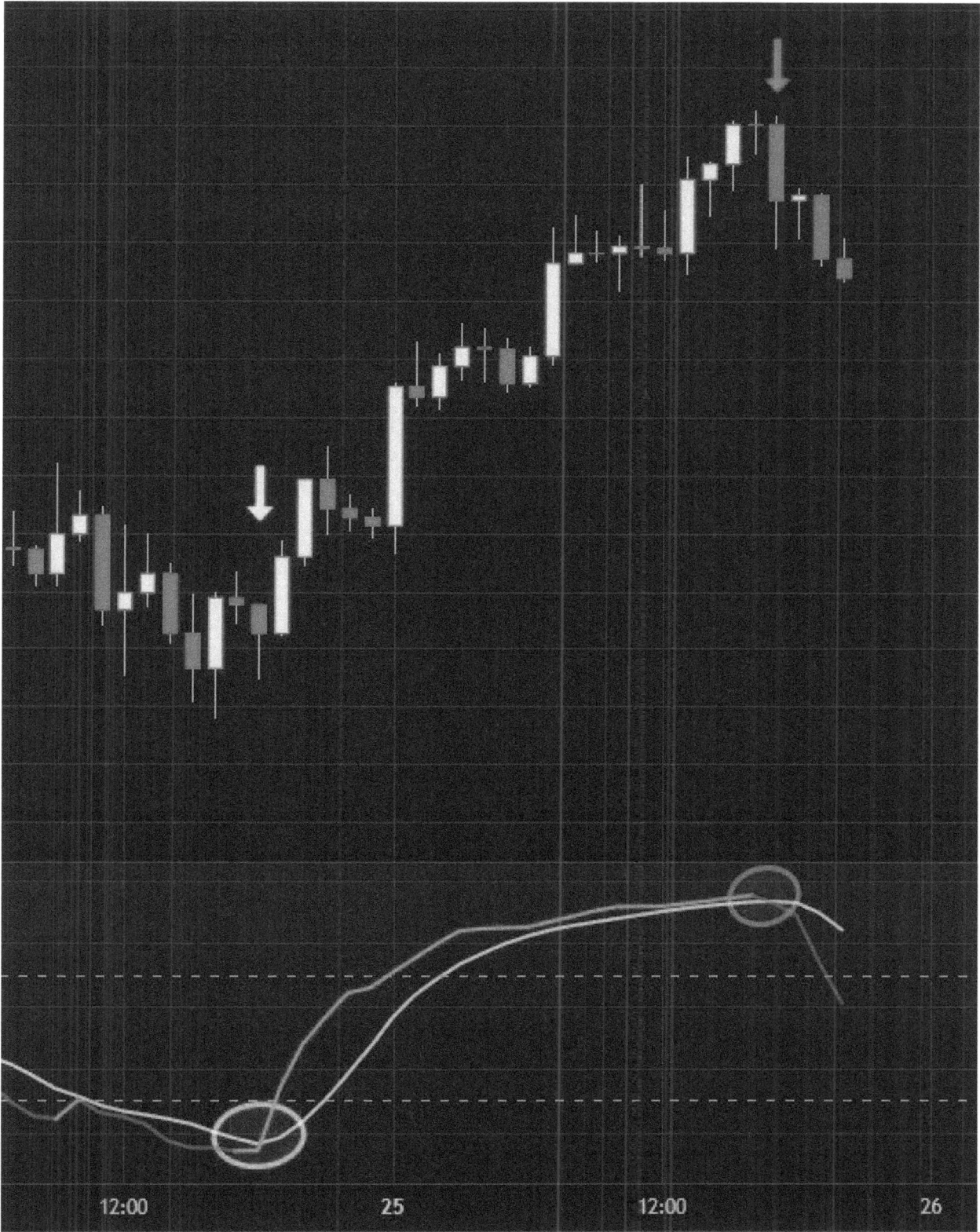

Example of a long trade using this indicator

Short Entry Signal:

- When the fast line (RMI) crosses below the slower moving average

Or

- The RMI changes to red color

Exit Short Signal

- When the fast line (RMI) crosses above the moving average

Or

- The RMI turns blue

Buy/Sell Signal #6: Quantitative Qualitative Estimation QQE

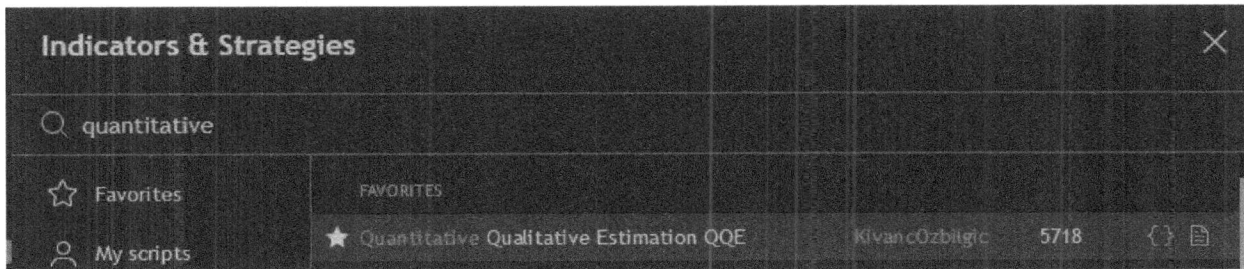

Search "Quantitative Qualitative Estimation" in the indicator search box on TradingView to find this indicator (author – KivancOzbilgic)

What is it?

This indicator combines the RSI with the two ATR lines, when the ATR lines cross this provides buy and sell signals. This indicator will display buy and sell signals on it making it easy to use.

You can also use overbought and oversold levels on this indicator for signals with below 30 being oversold and above 70 being overbought.

Buy Signal:

- When the fast line crosses above the slower line

Sell Signal

- When the fast line crosses below the slow line

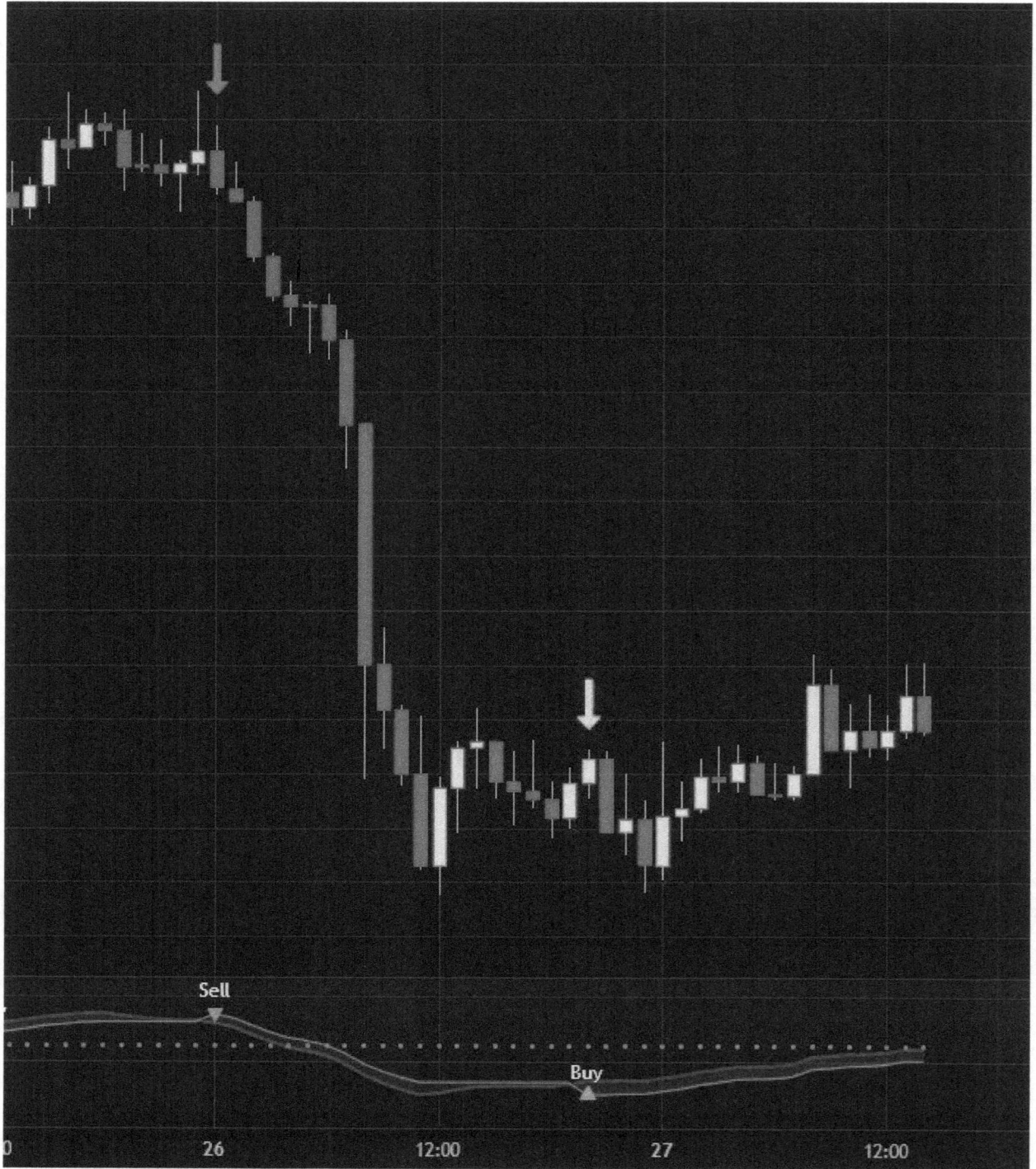

Example of buy and sell signals using this indicator

Buy/Sell Signal #7: Boom Hunter Pro

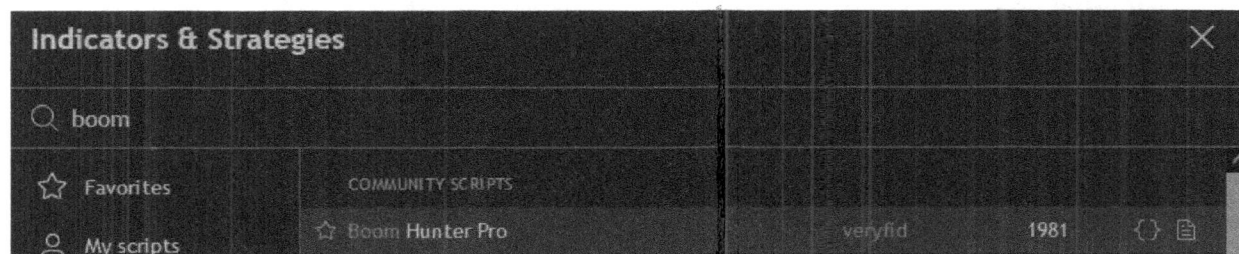

Search "Boom Hunter Pro" in the indicator search box on TradingView to find this indicator (Author – veryfid)

How it Works:

This is a oscillator displays two lines that cross over similar to a stochastic indicator but it uses a number of different calculations to produce overbought and oversold signals. This will display buy and sell signals as green and red dots.

Buy Signal:
- Green dots appear on the oscillator

Sell Signal:
- Red dots appear on the oscillator

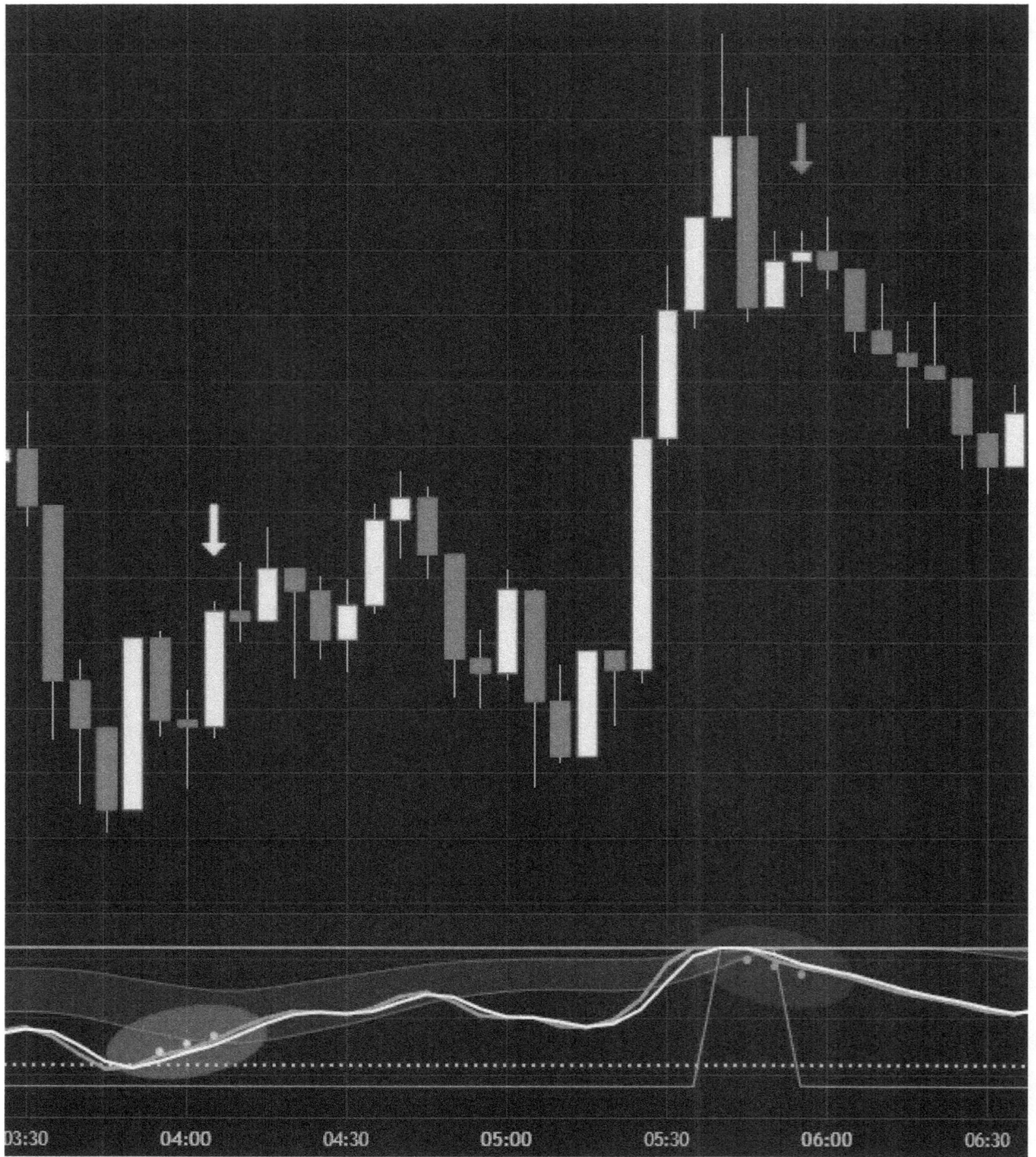

Example of buy signals (green circle) and sell signals (red circle) using the Boom Hunter Pro indicator

Buy/Sell Signal #8: [SK] Custom Klinger Oscillator

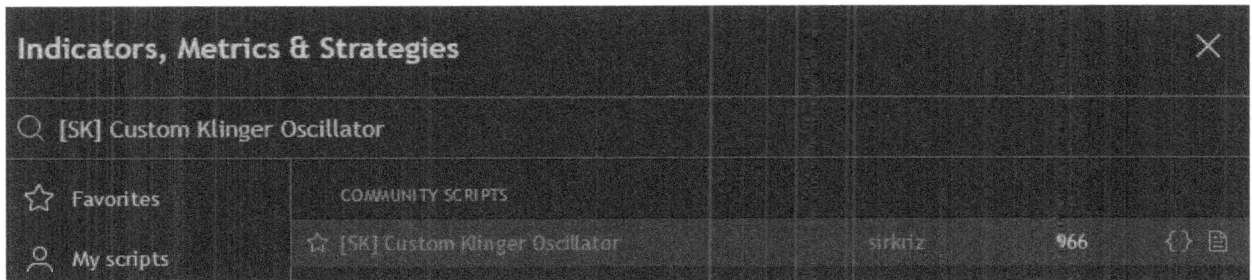

Indicators, Metrics & Strategies			✕
🔍 [SK] Custom Klinger Oscillator			
☆ Favorites	COMMUNITY SCRIPTS		
👤 My scripts	☆ [SK] Custom Klinger Oscillator	sirkriz 966	{} 📄

Search "[SK] Custom Klinger Oscillator" in the indicator search box on TradingView to find this indicator (Author: sirkriz)

How it Works:

This is a modified version of the Klinger osclillator. The Klinger oscillator is a volume based indicator and consists of two lines - one fast MA (moving average) and one slow.

Signals will be generated when the two lines crossover. The zero line on this indicator can also be used to confirm downtrends and uptrends.

Recommended Settings:

- Change the signal length to 12 to reduce false signals (uncheck the "use default values" box first).

Buy Signal:

- The fast MA crosses above the slower one
- The fast MA turns green

Sell Signal:

- The fast MA crosses below the slower
- The fast MA turns red

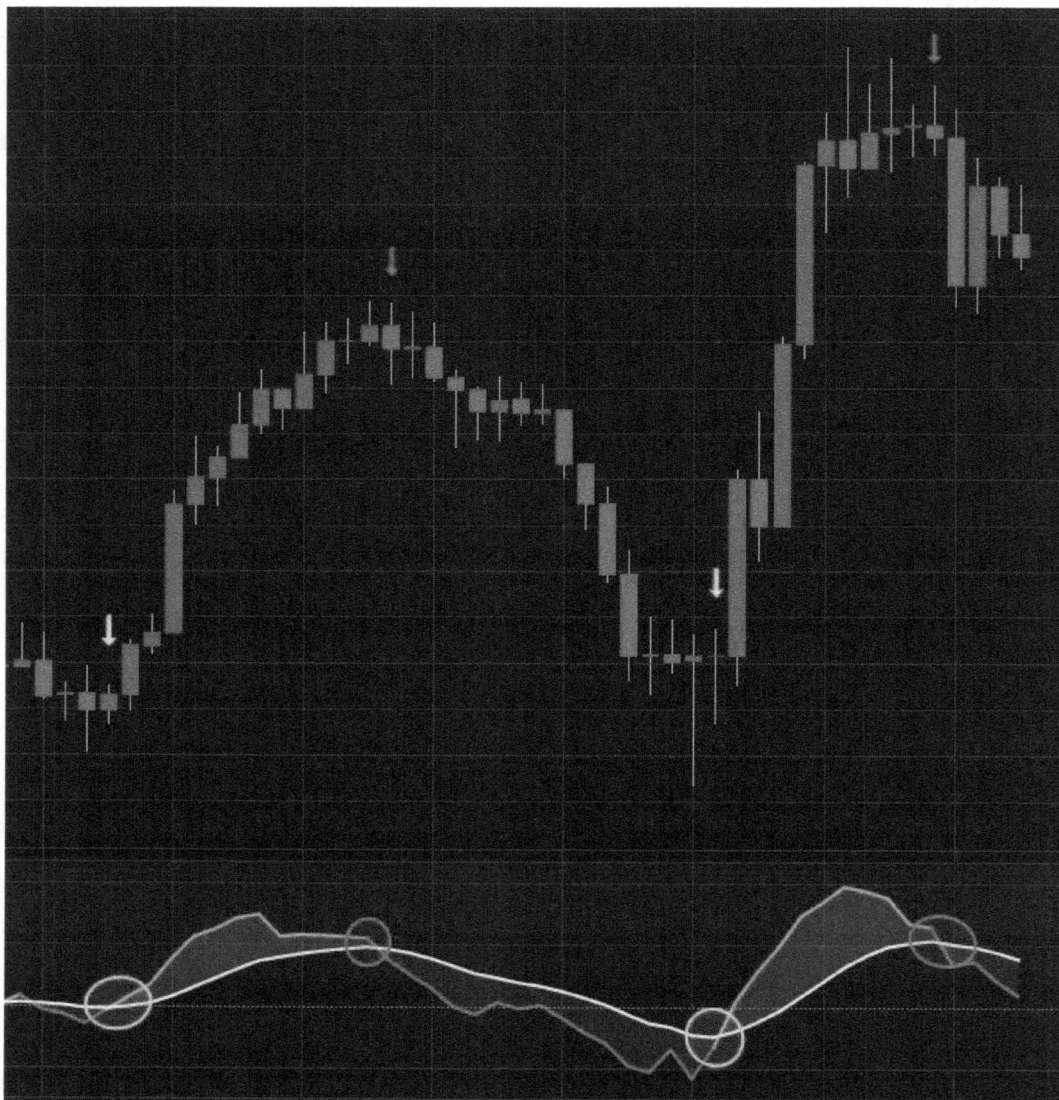

Example of buy signals (green circles) and sell signals (red circles) using the

[SK] Custom Klinger Oscillator

Chapter 4: Trend Indicator and Moving Average Buy/Sell Signals

In this chapter we'll be exploring how to generate buy and sell signals using a different trend indicators and moving averages. These indicators can be used to identify when a security is in an uptrend or downtrend and also provide accurate buy and sell signals.

The most common trend indicators are the moving averages. Moving averages lag the market because they are based on past prices. However, they are still one of the best ways to identify the direction of the market.

The most common moving average buy/sell signals are crossovers. A crossover occurs when a shorter-term moving average crosses above a longer-term moving average. This is considered a bullish signal and indicates that the market is in an uptrend.

Conversely, when a shorter-term moving average crosses below a longer-term moving average, this is considered a bearish signal and indicates that the market is in a downtrend. Another type of crossover occurs when price crosses a moving average, closing the candle above or below it. This is called a price crossover and can be used to generate buy and sell signals.

When using trend indicators and moving averages to generate buy and sell signals, it's important to use them in trending markets. You want to avoid using them in choppy or range-bound markets as they will generate a lot of false signals.

There are many different types of trend indicators and moving averages that can be used to generate buy and sell signals. The most important thing is to find an indicator that works well for you and that you're comfortable using.

What Is It?

This strategy uses the Hull moving average to generate buy/sell signals. A signal will occur when price crosses above or below the Hull moving average.

The Hull moving average is different from a traditional moving average because it is more responsive to recent price action. This makes it a great choice for day trading.

What are the best settings?

- HMA length: 60 period

Buy Signal:

- A buy signal occurs when price crosses above the Hull moving average

Sell Signal:

- A sell signal occurs when price crosses below the Hull moving average

Trend Indicator Buy/Sell Signal #2: SSL Hybrid

Search "SSL Hybrid" in the indicator search box on TradingView to find this indicator (author – Mihkel00)

How it Works:

This indicator is similar to a moving average but uses a combination of moving averages and ATR values to increase its accuracy. Like other trend confirmation indicators it will change colors, when indicating uptrends the SSL will turn blue and downtrends it will turn red.

The SSL indicator is a good trend confirmation indicator, as well as entries and exits. This indicator displays buy and sell signals as arrows, which can give you accurate entries and exits.

Recommended Settings:

- To make this indicator look cleaner on your chart, only set it to display the SSL moving average in the style settings

Buy Signal:

- The SSL line is blue
- Price is above the SSL line

Sell Signal:

- The SLL line is red
- Price is below the SSL line

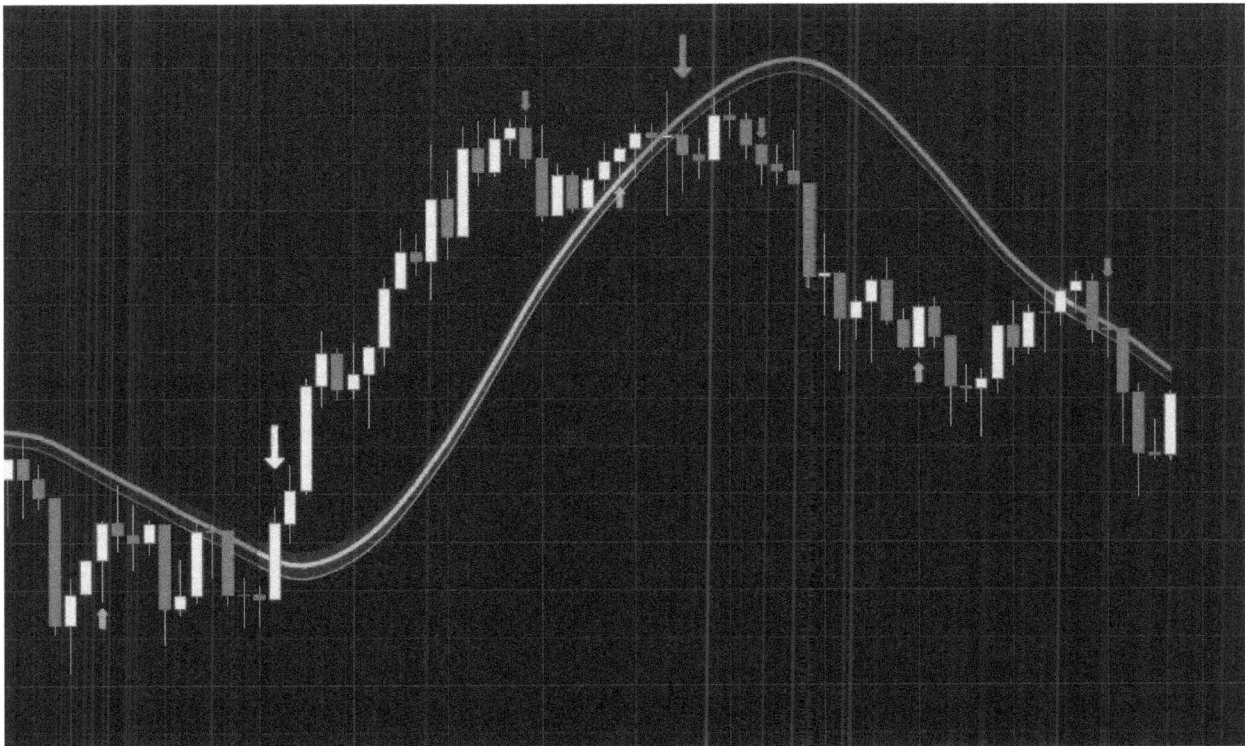

Example of a uptrend signal (green arrow) and downtrend signal (red arrow) using this indicator.

What is it?

This method uses the crossover of two VWMA (volume weight moving averages)to generate buy/sell signals. The VWMA is a moving average that gives more weight to recent volume this reduces lag and makes more accurate for crossovers.

What are the best settings?

The best settings for the VWMA Crossover method are:

- Fast VWMA: 10 period
- Slow VWMA: 21 period

Buy Signal:

- A buy signal occurs when the fast VWMA crosses above the slow VWMA.

Sell Signal:

- A sell signal occurs when the fast VWMA crosses below the slow VWMA

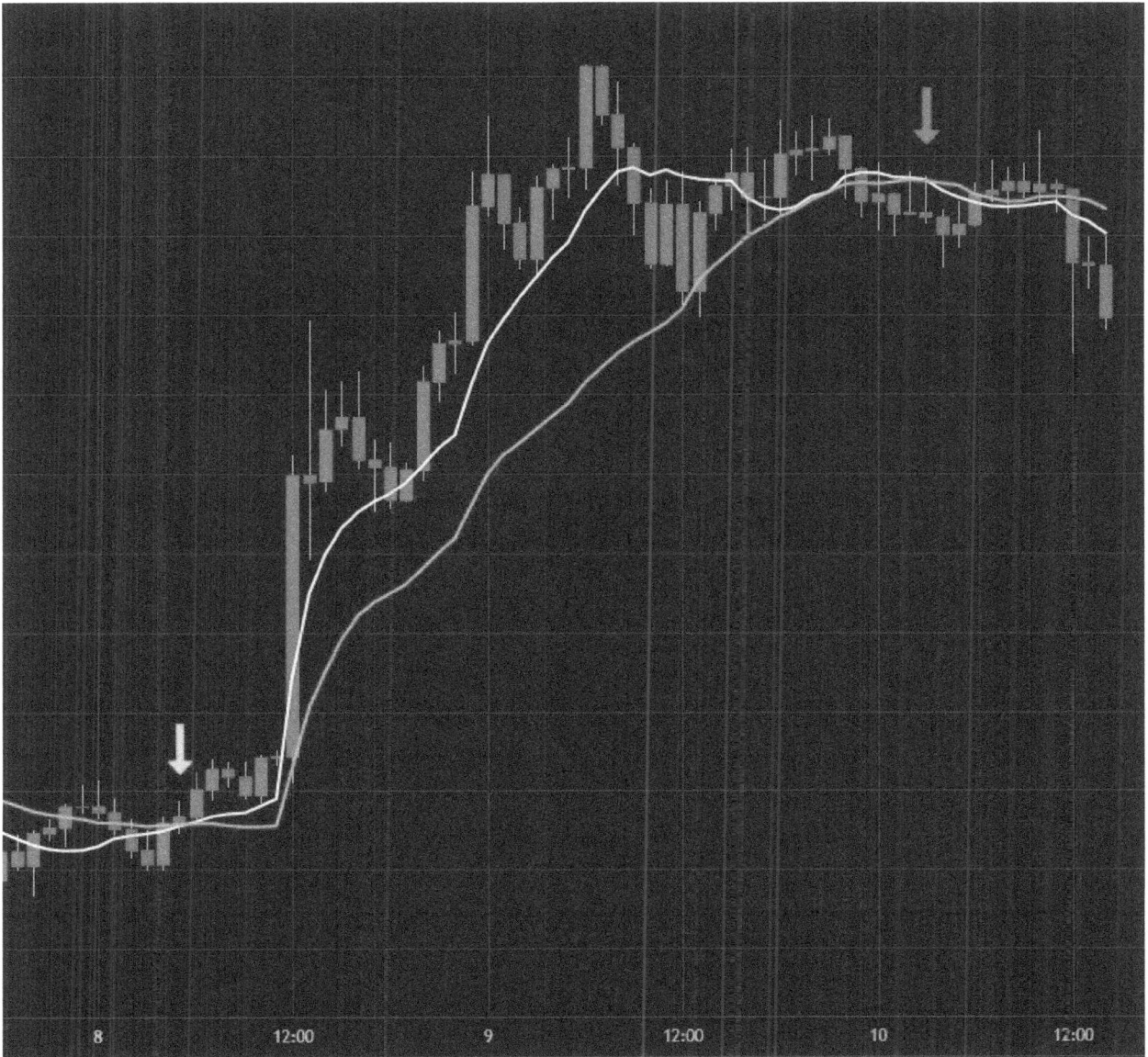

Example of buy and sell signals using this strategy

Trend Indicator Buy/Sell Signal #3: Trend Magic

Type "Trend Magic" in the indicator search box on TradingView to find this indicator (author: KivancOzbilgic).

How it Works:

This is an ATR based indicator that also uses the CCI in its calculations. This indicator appears as a single line on your chart, and changes color based on the CCI readings. When price is above the trend magic indicator and it is blue a uptrend is likely occurring. Likewise if price is below the TM and it is red, a downtrend is most likely occurring.

This is a good trend confirmation indicator that works well when combined with entry and exit signals from momentum indicators.

Recommended Settings

- Change the CCI to 50

Buy Signal:

- The TM is blue

- Price is above the TM line

Sell Signal:

- The TM is red

- Price is below the TM line

Trend Indicator Buy/Sell Signal #4: Pmax

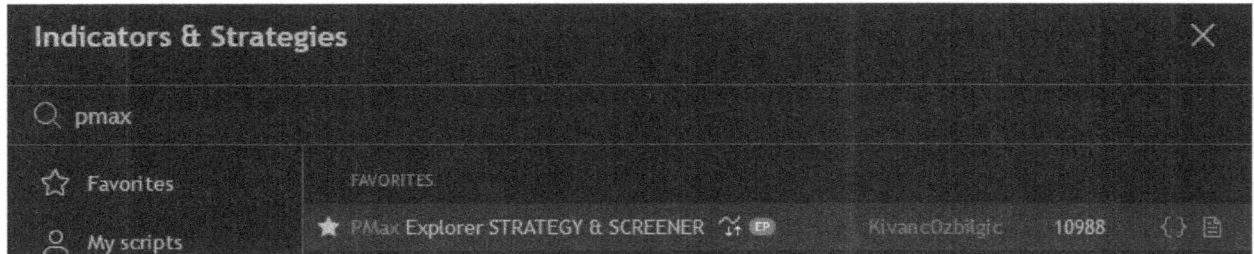

Indicators & Strategies   ✕

🔍 pmax

☆ Favorites   FAVORITES

👤 My scripts   ★ PMax Explorer STRATEGY & SCREENER 🎛 ⓔ   KivancOzbilgic   10988   {} 📄

Type "PMax Explorer" in the indicator search box on TradingView to find this indicator (author: KivancOzbilgic).

How it Works:

This indicator is a modified supertrend indicator which uses a combination of the ATR and moving averages. This indicator is designed to show trend reversals, and is a very good trend confirmation indicator.

The Pmax indicator is simple to use, and will tell you when a buy and sell signal occurs.

Indicator Buy Signal:

- The PMax turns green, and shows a buy signal

Indicator Sell Signal:

- The Pmax turns red and shows a sell signal

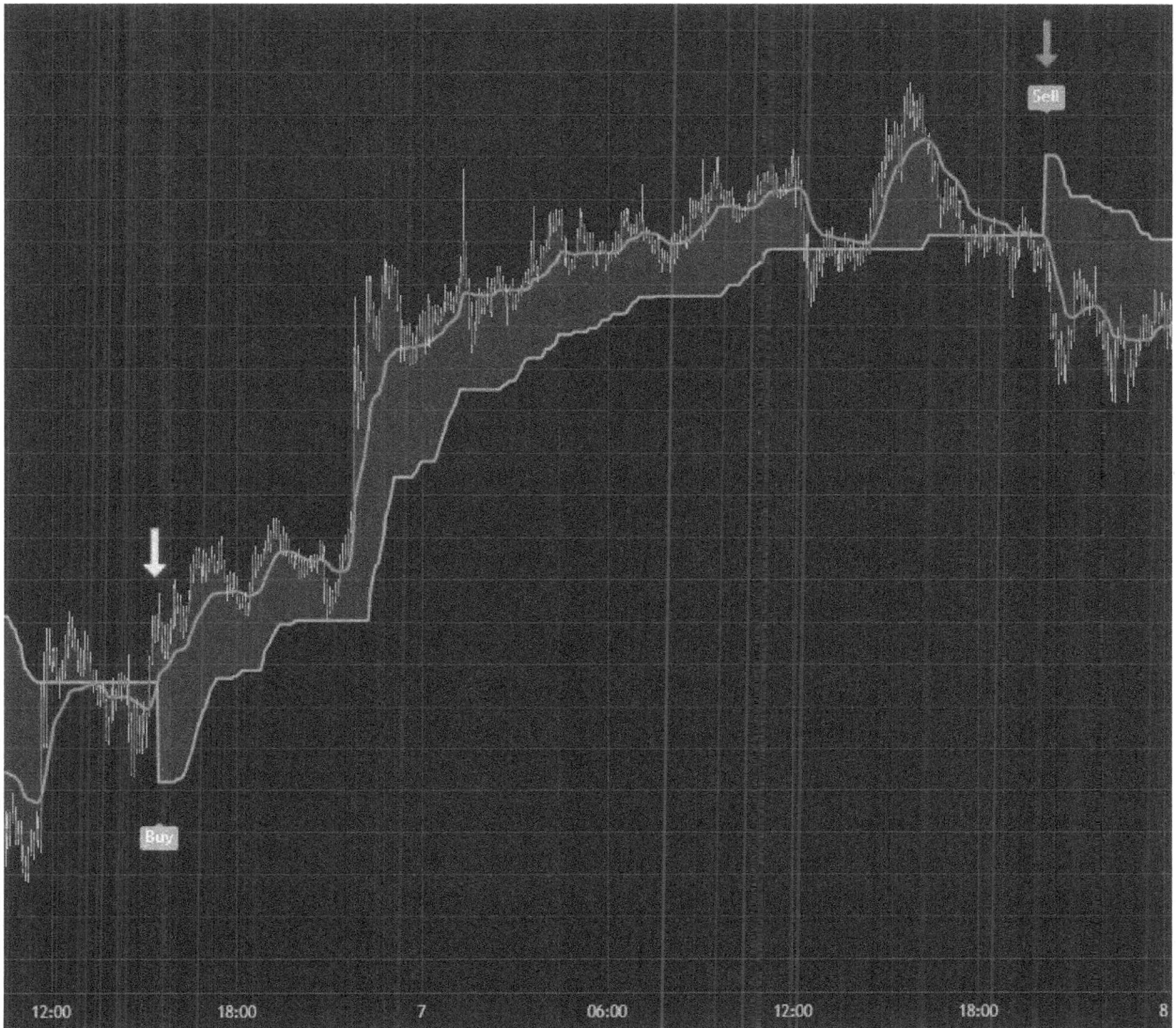

Example of buy (green arrow) and sell (red arrow) signals using this indicator

Trend Indicator Buy/Sell Signal #5: 500 EMA Cross

How It Works:

This method uses price closing above or below the 500 EMA to generate buy and sell signals. When price crosses the 500 EMA it accurately signals a trend change in the market. This is a good signal for swing trading since it is very infrequent but accurate.

Recommended Settings:

- EMA length: 500

Buy Signal:

- Price closes above the 500 EMA

Sell Signal:

- Price closes below the 500 EMA

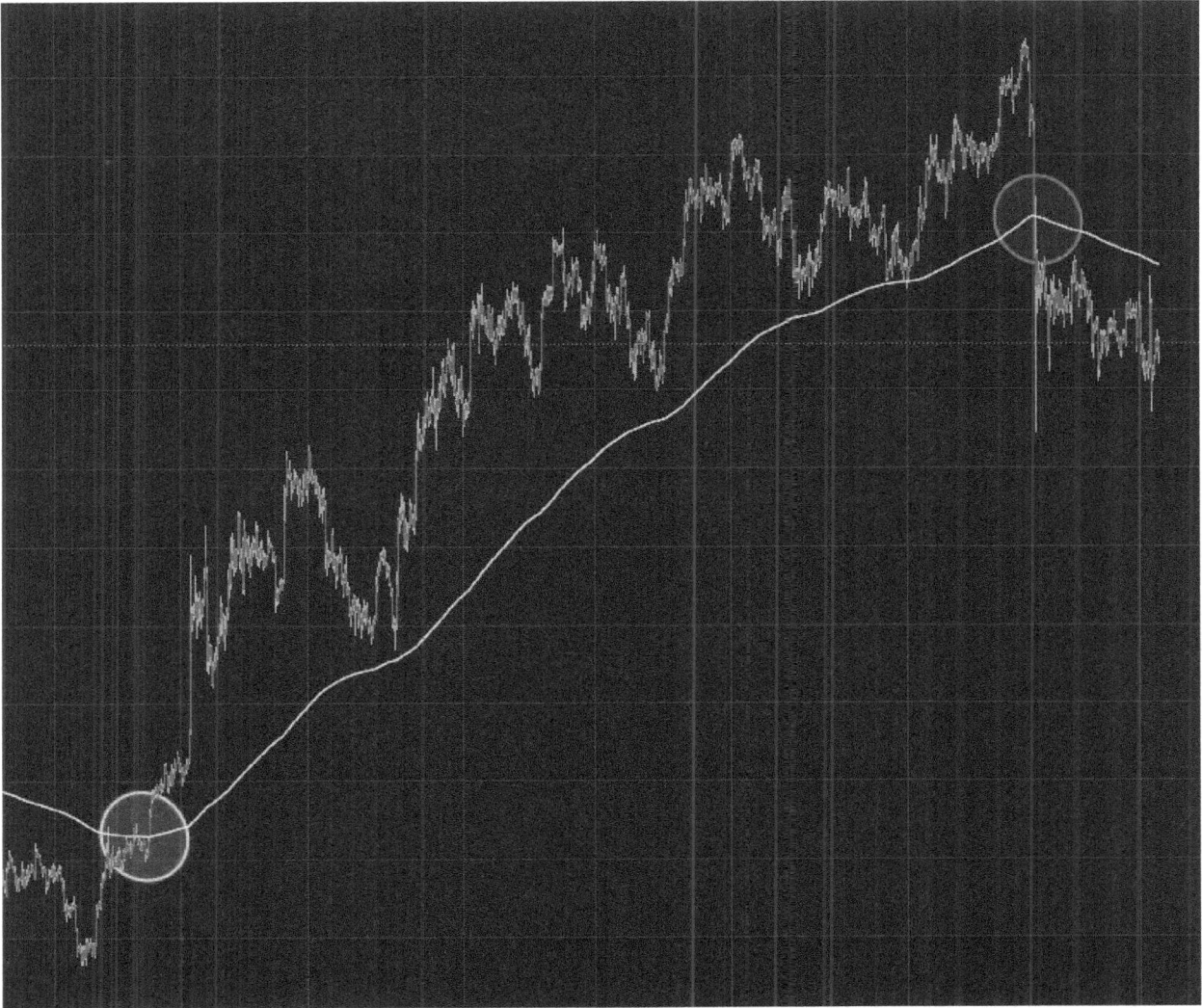

Example of buy (green circle) and sell (red circle) signals using this method

Trend Indicator Buy/Sell Signal #6: Gaussian Channel

Indicators, Metrics & Strategies ✕

🔍 gaussian

☆ Favorites   COMMUNITY SCRIPTS

👤 My scripts   ☆ Gaussian Channel [DW]   Donovan Wall   3635   {} 📄

Type "Gaussian Channel" in the indicator search box on TradingView to find this indicator (author: DonovanWall).

What is it?

This indicator is based on using multiple EMAs to produce a channel. When price is above the channel the market is likely in a uptrend and below a downtrend. Buy and sell signals occur when price touches the middle line of the channel.

Buy Signal:

- The GC is green and price touches the middle line

Sell Signal:

- The GC is red and touches the middle line

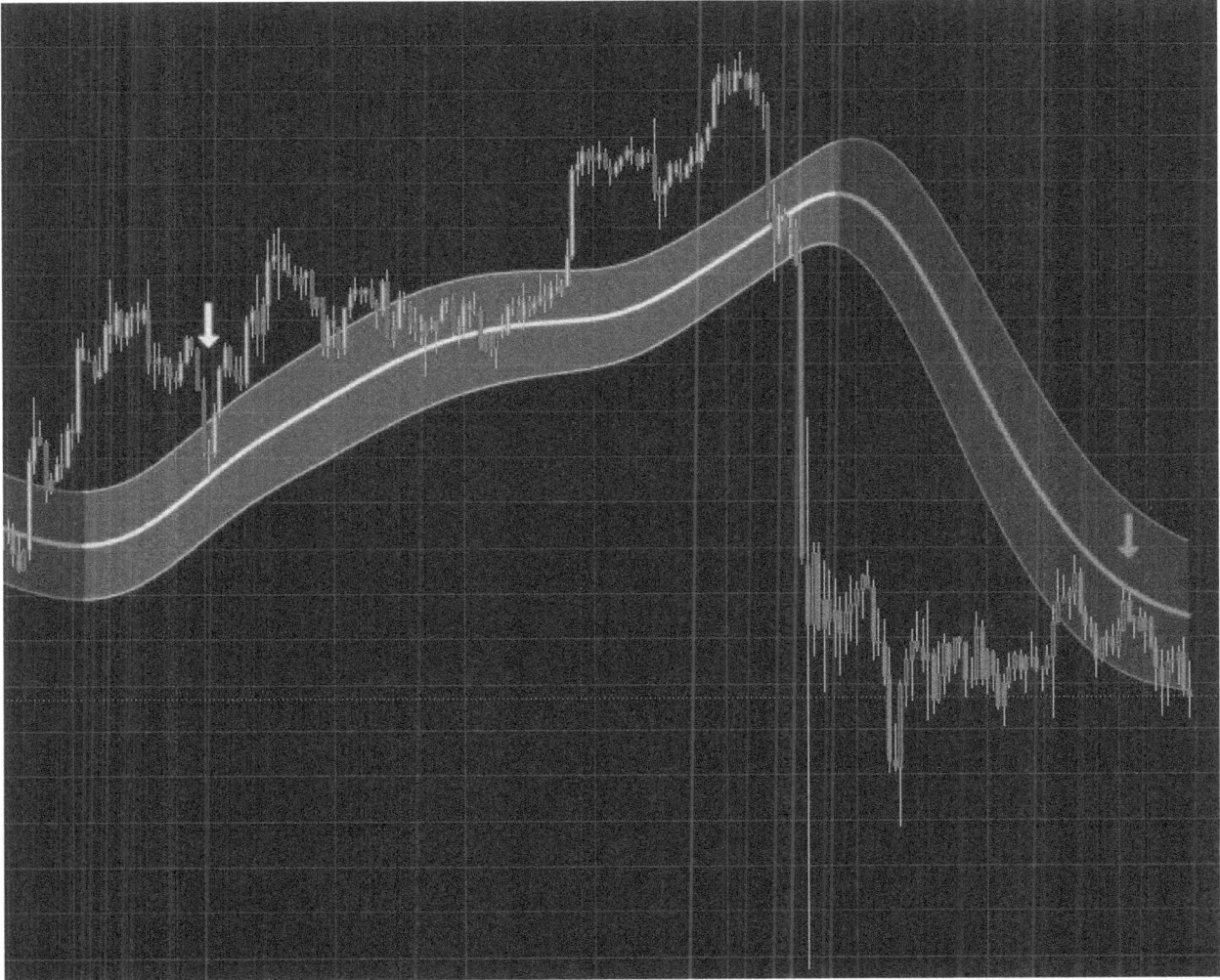

Example of buy (green arrow) and sell (red arrow) signals using this indicator

* 9 7 8 1 8 0 4 3 4 3 3 2 6 *